I0559186

OUT OF THE DARKNESS AND OTHER ANIMAL TAILS

Lessons in Compassion and Healing from the Animal World

ROSE DE DAN

These are my memories, from my perspective, and I have tried to represent events as faithfully as possible.

ISBN 979-8-9909803-1-0 (paperback)

ISBN 979-8-9909803-0-3 (e-book)

Copyright © 2024 Rose De Dan. All Rights Reserved.

No part of this book may be used or reproduced by any means, graphic, electronic, or mechanical, including photocopying, photographing, recording, taping, or by any information storage retrieval system without the written permission of the publisher except in the case of brief quotations embodied in critical articles and reviews.

Cover Photo (Woods): Johannes Plenio

Cover Design: 100Covers

Layout/Design: Rose De Dan and Vellum

Silhouette Art/Animal Footprints: Dingbat fonts Animal Tracks (Andrew D. Taylor), Bats (Woodcutter Manero), Birds of a Feather and Zoologic (Iconian Fonts), DjHorses (Donna Morse), and Shutterstock

Photographs: Rose De Dan unless otherwise noted.

Publisher: Wild Reiki and Shamanic Healing LLC, www.ReikiShamanic.com

INSPIRATIONS

Handsome feline Shakespurr was an energy-healing client of mine for years and became the purring muse whose unwavering support and love for stories inspired me to create more "tails."

His person, Lauren Psomosthithis, would tell me that Shakespurr would show up to listen to me tell stories while she was editing videos for Wild Reiki and Shamanic Healing or teaching online classes, and created a video of him for me.

Shakespurr was a major inspiration for the original Storytelling for Animals and People audio series from which the stories in this book were collected, along with parrot Max, who appears later in "A Story for African Grey Parrot Max."

I am grateful to them both for raising my awareness that All My Relations like to hear the stories, too!

Shakespurr listening to my voice while Ceasar snoozes.

CONTENTS

PACHAMAMA'S AMBASSADOR

LIFE ON THE EDGE

PREFACE

Considering how many stories I have told over the years, it took a while for me to realize that the animals wanted to hear the stories, too. Students often shared with me that their animal companions would gather to watch my videos, listen to the classes, and generally show up to be part of the energy.

One student told me she had carefully closed the door to the room so that she could listen without disturbance to our first call for Reiki class. However, as soon as the call started, her animal companions began trying to tear the door down to get in. And they insisted on being part of every call going forward, even though the stories were interspersed with teaching. One of those listeners was cat Shakespurr.

The final jump in awareness came from parrot Max who lived at Cougar Mountain Zoo and made it clear that he enjoyed listening to a good story.

So I reached out to the animals and asked what they wanted. They said, "Gather the people and the animals so that we may sit together in the energy that unites us and hear the tales of animals as teachers and guides. Call upon the ancient ties that unite us, that we may remember together, gain inspiration together, and move forward as one."

Storytelling for Animals and People premiered as an audio-only presentation on April 13, 2017. Most of the stories shared over many months were original, written just for the series, while a few had previously been published on my blog.

All of those stories* are now gathered here, in the order in which they first debuted.

And for each story, I chose the appropriate animal track (when possible) to represent the footprints that All Our Relations leave in our hearts and on our lives.

Enjoy!

Rose De Dan

---

* I opened the series with a reading of "The Cat Who Walked by Himself" from *Just So Stories* by Rudyard Kipling; the only story that does not appear in this collection. There are many stories told of how People first welcomed animals into their lives and homes; Rudyard Kipling's version made a huge impact on me as a child. I choose it for the *Storytelling* series because its energy reflects the many threads connecting us to our Animal Relatives. Although Kipling's story is no longer copyright protected, I did not feel right including it here. I hope that readers will choose to seek it out in print, or, perhaps in the audio/video version of Storytelling.

CONNECTIONS

Storytelling #1

LADY JANE

As a child, I always remember us having dogs. The dog I recall most vividly was Lady Jane—she was a part of my life for as long as I could remember.

She was a dog of uncertain parentage—my mother called her a Heinz 57—but she definitely had some spaniel in her. Her tail swept out in a plume of fur, and she had liquid brown eyes.

Mom would tell us that before Lady Jane came to live with us, she was feral, roaming the marshes around where we lived and hunting the many rabbits that called our neighborhood home. She was very shy—no one could get near her.

My mother resolved to try to rescue her, and over time, with the help of tasty food and treats, Lady Jane began to come closer to her.

During that in-between place between being feral and becoming our family dog, Lady Jane did not want to let our mother out of her sight. Mom told us that she would get in the car to go on an errand, and Lady Jane would follow, running as fast as she could to keep up; she would have to return to the house with her errand undone because Lady Jane simply would not give up. She seemed to be willing to follow Mom forever, wherever she went.

Eventually, Mom coaxed Lady Jane into the house, and she became domesticated on the surface. But Lady Jane's heart was still wild and only belonged to our mother—she tolerated everyone else, but she loved Mom.

Lady Jane shares her food bowl with kitten Scruffy.

I grew up in an unusual household. In most families, the kids plead for a puppy or kitten and vehemently promise to take care of him/her if only they could have one. I don't recall ever pleading to adopt an animal as a child. Instead, our mother worked on Dad. The poor man was allergic to animals and had to go for weekly shots to survive.

Once the animal in question became part of our household, Mom rarely paid attention or cared for them; it was all left up to my sisters and me. Over the years, as you might imagine, othat caused some resentment as we scrubbed the chicken coop, cleaned the aviary and litter box, walked the dogs, and fed and watered everyone. None of the animals were ours; they were all with us because of Mom. A number of them gravitated to us, and we did love them, but Lady Jane only ever truly loved Mom, even though we were the ones who took care of her.

Our parents divorced, and we moved to another house. A lot of things changed. Mom took a job an hour and a half away from home, and as the eldest, much more of the household care fell on my shoulders and those of my sisters.

Then, Mom began staying in the city and only coming home on weekends. We had a housekeeper who cared for us during the day, but I was in charge at night. I was 15.

Lady Jane had made her den under our mother's bed during this time. That was where she stayed, and each day, getting her to come out to eat and go outside was a struggle. We would have to reach under and grab her collar, and often, she would snap at us when we tugged. She also smelled awful.

One morning, as one of my sisters narrowly avoided getting bitten in her efforts to get Lady Jane out from under the bed, I'd had enough. I called my mother and told her that Lady Jane was suffering and that she needed to be put to sleep. I had never told my mother that she must do something in my entire life since she had some anger issues, but I realized that we could no longer deal with whatever was going on with Lady Jane. Someone had to be the adult, and if my mother was not going to be one, then I had to do it.

My mother got upset, and I had to argue with her. Finally, she angrily said, "Well, if you are going to do it, do it; just don't tell me about it." At that moment, I truly realized that I was on my own. Lady Jane had just become my complete responsibility. I was 16 years old.

I made the appointment, and our housekeeper drove Lady Jane and me to the vet. It was just the two of us in the exam room we were escorted to. The assistant told me to go to the front desk, and while I was standing there, I was presented with Lady Jane's collar. The instant it touched my hand, I knew she was gone, and I broke down in tears. I just couldn't help it. I think what bothered me the most was that Lady Jane died alone, without the one person that she loved more than anyone else in the whole wide world—my mother.

It took me years to understand the complex and very messed up person that was my mother, and what she must have experienced as a child to make her who she was as an adult, and even more years to forgive her.

But forgiveness was never an issue for Lady Jane. She loved Mom unconditionally and faithfully. Of us all, only Lady Jane realized that the healing energy Mom needed most was love—and Lady Jane offered all that she had to give.

OUT OF THE DARKNESS

I n my early days as a student of shamanism, I went for a 10-day training at a beautiful wooded retreat in southern California. Sounds lovely, doesn't it? Afterward, I promised myself I would never do that again.

Imagine 10 days spent in the company of 50 or so folks with major energetic and emotional baggage that they didn't know they needed to get rid of, where every day drama and chaos reign in class (a story for another time), and hucha (heavy energy) is flying everywhere.

Now imagine having sacred space open 24/7 with no hope of escape. Next, imagine that you have no place to go for privacy since you have two roommates with no boundaries and one entity—an entity that the roommate said "no" to letting go of during class, "no" in the evening as we were trying to go to sleep (which of course was when the entity began to gear up and frighten her), and "no" until 3 a.m. when I finally said enough and dragged both roommates out of bed to have the entity removed since it was not letting any of us sleep.

My revenge? I made my roommates sing, "We're off to see the wizard," while marching them through the darkened meadow on our way to wake up the teaching assistants, who, needless to say, were not too happy to be dragged out of bed, either.

Ten days in sacred space is a lot for anyone. It will surely drag out all the major dirty laundry you stuffed into the closet long ago, and I was no exception.

I was not used to spending so much time with so many people *and* their issues, and I don't think I realized just how much my emotional balance depended on being able to connect with and touch animals. And now I was marooned in the woods with wildly erratic energy and very unstable people who were throwing their emotional Samsonite everywhere, and not a dog or cat in sight.

However, there was beautiful scenery aplenty. At lunch, I would steal away from the group and sit on a little dock that extended out into a gorgeous sunlit lake where fish lived, waterfowl waded, and dragonflies hovered. I would desperately try to find a little peace and balance. But I could not hold on to the tranquility for long—another shamanic practitioner would join me, and the moment would be lost.

One night, as I walked by myself along a dirt path through the woods, I hit my breaking point. I felt completely alone without the animal friends that I was used to seeking comfort from. I'd heard that there were bears in the area, and I was so far gone that, at that moment, I would have gladly welcomed the company of a bear.

I felt anguish rise up in me, a pain so deep that it felt like my heart was breaking; I was alone, and there was no one that I trusted to comfort me. I stopped walking and just stood in the middle of the path. I felt my heart crack open, and a silent, anguished cry went out into the darkness of the heavily wooded forest—a cry of yearning for a cat to comfort me. I felt despair that in the middle of nowhere, there would be no one to answer my call.

And then—like something from a fairy tale—out of the darkness, a cat came running, headed straight toward me. I fell to my knees in the dirt and opened my arms and heart wide to receive him. He ran into my arms, and as I fiercely hugged him, I cried tears of gratitude, awe, and joy into his fur. He purred comfort into my broken heart, covering me with his scent and strength. And just like that, balance was restored.

I repeatedly told this mystery cat how grateful I was for his gift and shared information on which cabin I was staying in should he wish to visit. I don't know how long we spent together, but I felt more like myself again when we parted.

The next morning, I asked the people running the retreat center if they knew of a cat who lived in the woods, and I described him. They looked at me as if I had two heads, and I began to think that perhaps, in my moment of shamanic disintegration, I had imagined our encounter. And then the man said, "That's Charlie, the camp cat, but he doesn't hang out with the visitors; he's pretty aloof." And then it was my turn to look at them in disbelief. Aloof? The cat who allowed himself to be hugged to my heart and showered me with purrs and rubs?

Later that day, Charlie stopped by the cabin. He did not come in—he didn't want to hang out with the roommates either—he just came by to check on me and make sure I was ok.

From then on, the wildlife in the area also made themselves known to me. Quail began to hang around the cabin, and their softly murmured conversations were soothing. An elusive bobcat let me see him as he darted through the brush. A herd of deer passed through the meadow in front of me.

And every night, after my roommates were asleep, a white cricket would creep out onto the hearth and join me in gazing into the dancing flames of the fire. He kept vigil with me, and I realized—thanks to Charlie and our incredible moment in the woods—that I am never alone, the animals are always with me, and they will always answer a call from the heart, just as I will always answer theirs.

FOR THE LOVE OF ANIMALS

Storytelling #2

ANIMAL MEDICINE CARD READING

I asked if I should pull a medicine card and was told yes. I don't know what made me think of it. And it's pretty funny because when I got the deck out, I felt strongly that there was a card in there that was intended as a message both for myself and, shall we say, related to this particular call.

As I shuffled, I could feel the card calling to me; it was very easy to pick out which one it was. Just before I turned it over, I said to myself, "Gosh, I hope it's not Bat." And sure enough, it was Bat. You might be wondering why I was worried. I have nothing against bats—I love them. I think they're wonderful beings, but from a shamanic perspective, they represent shamanistic death. I tend to think of the Bat card as similar to the Tower card in a Tarot deck where everything kind of blows up and falls apart. Bat represents an initiation, and it can be rough. The idea of shamanic initiation is to break down all the notions of self that we hold (our ego) and get through to who we really are on the soul level. And that often involves darkness, which is Bat's realm, and confronting your fears.

As I pondered this, I thought of Cave Bat. In our last call, I read Rudyard Kipling's story "The Cat Who Walked by

Himself," which included the messenger Bat, who hung upside down in the cave and brought information to Cat. Hanging upside down symbolizes birth and rebirth in the Tarot (the Hanged Man). So, generally speaking, the Bat symbolizes the need for the end of some way of life that no longer suits your new growth pattern. Speaking for myself, I realized that my spirit allies were asking me to step into a new way of bringing this energy, this new way of being, into the world; we each do that in who we are. The stories here celebrate the animals, our connection and relationship to them, and how they support and inspire growth.

When they [the animals] share with us who they are, they also show us the way back to who we are, which, of course, is very much needed at this time and helps call us back. Remembering.

So, in honor of that and in honor of the animals, this evening, I will do my very best to tell the stories and call forth the energy in the way that they wish to have it represented.

FOR THE LOVE OF ANIMALS

My love of animals and desire to protect All My Relations started at a young age. I was an odd child. When we went through the drive-thru at the bank, they always handed out dog biscuits, which I would gnaw on to the horror of my grandmother--she would scold me and tell me that I would get worms from them. I knew that was not true since why would we feed them to the dogs? And birds ate worms, so they couldn't be bad for you.

My desire to sample the animals' food extended to some new treats we had gotten for the cats. They were chicken-flavored puffs and looked good, so I had one. They tasted great.

My father was a dentist, my mother was a dental hygienist, and their practice was attached to our house. I knew the dental assistants and receptionist well and decided to test my new taste sensation on them. I knew they would not eat them if they knew they were cat treats, so I told them how great this snack was and offered them one without the bag. They loved them. Then I told them, and it was comical to see how upset they were to realize they had just eaten cat treats. I thought it was all silly. If the ingredients were the same as human food, why couldn't we eat them? What difference did a label make? My parents disagreed; however, I think they may have been secretly amused since I didn't get punished, just told not to do it again.

The same lazy Susan that housed the dog and cat foods also saw a lot of mouse activity. It seemed that my father was always engaged in a struggle to try to get rid of the mice. Sadly, our cats did not seem interested in the problem; if they were, they were not making much of a difference. At the time, I was too young to understand what it meant when my parents finally resorted to putting out poison.

I think my first awareness of death was the day that a mouse who had consumed the poison bait staggered out into the middle of the kitchen floor and died right in front of me. What happened next went down in family history and is still told to this day.

I was horrified. Scooping the little mouse up in my hands, I knew I had to bring him to my mother since she always helped our animals when they got sick. That meant I had to go into the office during office hours, which I was not supposed to do unless there was an emergency. To me, a sick mouse *was* an emergency, so I marched in with the mouse resting in my cupped hands. I made it past my father, who was working on a patient in the first room, and to the second room, where my mother was working on her patient.

When my mother told the next part of the story, it always went like this, "You appeared at the patient's shoulder, and passing the dead mouse directly under the woman's chin, you tearfully said, 'Mommy, make it better.'" Then my mother would add, "Thankfully, my patient was lying so far back that she could not see what you had in your hands, and I was able to whisk you both back into the house before she could see the mouse."

After that experience, I believe my parents returned to using the standard mousetraps.

Years later, after my parents were divorced and my father continued his practice at our old house, the mouse problem persisted.

As an adult, I suggested that my father use a humane trap so the mouse could be set free somewhere else. I don't know if how upset I was as a child about that first dead mouse still lingered in his mind after all those years, but he told me later that he had done just that, but that it was challenging freeing them from the trap. I asked him why, and he said the glue was very sticky.

My father was not an animal person, and the fact that he would go to so much trouble to make me happy meant a lot. I winced, thinking how sore the mouse's feet might be after being forcibly removed from the glue, and I blessed each one for not biting my father since it must have been scary, too. I told my father that I truly appreciated his efforts and gently suggested that a different type of trap might be easier for him and the mouse in the future.

THE FIELD

I grew up in what could loosely have been considered an urban setting, but it was really semi-rural. At the time, the city of Linwood had about 6,000 residents—small enough that with my parents having a professional practice, everyone seemed to know who I was. Getting away with anything was nearly impossible.

One block down the street was an open field that led to the tall grasses of the marsh and the bay. Nearby was Off's Pond, where we often walked to feed the ducks and geese. There were also great blue herons that nested there.

The field contained an old shed that had fallen into disrepair. Not much was left of its roof, but it apparently offered some shelter since the mourning doves loved to congregate in it.

A favorite pastime of mine was to quietly approach the shed. When I was near enough to be heard, I would begin speaking to them by cooing as they did. I did it well enough that they would answer back, and I could stand in there with them just overhead for a few peaceful moments. If I were unsuccessful, I would hear the sudden thunder of their wings as they fled perceived danger.

In the field, wildlife abounded, including smaller forms of butterflies, toads, caterpillars, sow bugs, and praying mantis egg cases—there was always something or someone to discover.

Looking back through the years, I don't recall having to let anyone know where I was going or when I would be back—a freedom I treasured. I spent a lot of time turning over rocks and stones to see who lived underneath. Usually, I discovered crickets, but I always hoped to discover a snake.

At the time, I was reading books about naturalists, and in those days, that meant being a collector. So I would bring the crickets home and place them in a tank where I kept them alive with lettuce and water. At night, their chirping songs lulled me to sleep.

One day, my big moment happened. I overturned a rock, and a garter snake slithered out. Even though I had never held a snake before, I captured it with a cry of delight. The snake immediately coiled around my arm, and thus intertwined, I marched triumphantly home.

Sadly for me, my parents were away. My mother would have celebrated my great discovery and helped me prepare a proper home. Instead, I was met by my grandmother, who was horrified. I did manage to get the snake in a tank, but she insisted it had to be kept outside. I visited him the next morning before school, but when I came home, he was gone.

My grandmother said that she took it to someone who told her it was poisonous, so she let it go. I knew she was not telling me the truth since we didn't have any poisonous snakes in our area, and I also knew a garter snake when I saw one. I was grumpy about the loss for days, but eventually forgave her. Few people shared my passion for spending time with animals of all kinds. My mother later told me that my grandmother was so afraid the snake would find its way back to us that she drove the poor thing two towns away to release it. I sure hope it found a good place to live.

One day, the unthinkable happened. I walked to what I considered my private nature reserve and my animal friends, and facing me was a large sign proclaiming the property for sale for development. I knew that meant that I was going to lose all my animal friends, and they were going to lose their homes. Then I got mad. I decided that I would take the sign down. Maybe if no one saw the sign, it would not be sold.

The sign was made of wood and was tall and very heavy. I worked and worked at wiggling the posts in an effort to topple it, but realized I was simply not big enough or strong enough to lift it by myself.

So, I went down the street to my friend Janet's house and offered to pay her a dollar if she would help me take down the sign. We knew it was probably against the law and we could get in trouble, but we both loved the field (well, maybe I loved it more). In any case, she agreed to help, and after much effort, we finally toppled it. As I recall, we had to do this several more times, and amazingly, we didn't get caught doing this in broad daylight.

Sadly, despite our valiant young efforts, the land was sold, the mourning dove shelter was torn down, the land was scraped clean of all living beings, and the houses began to go up. I mourned the loss for quite a while.

Many years later, happily, Off's Pond and the marsh are still untouched.

The last time I visited, I walked to the edge of the marsh where it meets the pond and was able to quietly approach the great blue heron that called it home. Some of the wild magic of my childhood still remained.

CAT SCRIMMAGE

My roommate woke me from a sound sleep. I looked at the clock; it was 1 a.m. With some urgency, she said, "The cats are all gathered in the kitchen and staring at the cabinet. It is very strange, and it is creeping me out."

Going downstairs, I discovered it was indeed, as she said. Six cats were gathered in a semicircle, and all of them had their gaze intensely focused on one cabinet door. I listened but did not hear anything. Clearly, however, they did.

I opened the cabinet door and gazed at the cereal boxes. They looked as unassuming as they usually did. However, when I moved one, I discovered the source of their interest: a young mouse had fallen between the boxes and was trying to get out. The scrabbling sound of his claws on the boxes must have alerted the cats.

Just as I realized what the problem was, but before my slightly sleep-fogged brain could come up with a solution, the mouse decided that leaving was the best course of action. The only way open was outward, so the mouse jumped out of the cabinet.

I panicked; the poor little guy did not stand a chance on the floor with the eager cats. Looking down, I tried to see where he had gone, as did the cats. I couldn't see him anywhere...The exact moment that I realized the mouse was hanging on for dear life to the front of my shirt, he lost his grip and fell to the floor, right into the middle of what was now a circle of cats.

What happened next must have looked like some demented version of a hockey scrum with cats as I dropped to the floor and dove for the mouse. Somehow, I managed to emerge from the huddle with the mouse in my hands. Oddly, he seemed unfazed by the whole experience; perhaps he was simply frozen with fear.

Much to the disappointment of the cats, I decided that outside was the best place for the cute little guy. When I placed him on the ground at my feet, I thought for sure he would fearfully dart off under the shed. Nope, instead, he plunked himself down on his tiny little haunches, right between my feet, and proceeded to have a good wash-up—apparently, his fur needed some grooming after all the excitement. Standing there with him, I was touched that he would consider someone so huge to be safe. However, my cats would have said that prey isn't smart, just tasty!

A GANDER JUST KNOWS

Last time, I told a story about an extremely intense 10-day training at a beautiful wooded retreat in southern California. I mentioned that there was a lot of drama and chaos daily, with hucha flying everywhere; sacred space was open 24/7, which meant that you were doing your personal work even in your sleep.

Early in the class, we did an exercise involving deeply personal work in partnership with another student. As part of the process of clearing stuck energy we shared our "story" around the issue with our partner. It is profoundly intimate work, and trust is involved in sharing how you are most vulnerable. A lot of heavy energy is also called up in the process, some of which hit the proverbial shamanic fan the following day.

One of the students took the floor to apologize to the class, his shamanic partner, and his girlfriend. I listened with disbelief as this man publicly confessed that during the exercise the previous day, he had become strongly attracted to the woman who had been his partner. His shamanic partner was as appalled by all this as the girlfriend with whom the man had come to the training. Both women were deeply embarrassed by the quantity of dirty laundry being dumped out in front of the class.

Afterward, somehow, I ended up in conversation with the girlfriend, discussing how to clear energetic patterns related to the incident and their relationship, which apparently was not great.

We were outside, and while walking, my attention was drawn to a very large gander who had quite a large flock of lady geese all to himself. Members of our shamanic class were heading to lunch, and I watched as the gander calmly allowed everyone to pass by without incident.

Suddenly, there was a huge honk; the gander flashed his wings open wide, charging straight for the boyfriend who had cheated in his heart. That male goose didn't care that the boyfriend was a different species; he recognized the energy of a potential rival and was having none of it!

PERU STORIES

Storytelling #3

JOURNEY TO MACHU PICCHU

In 2002, I traveled to the sacred valley of Peru with a group of folks who had also trained in Peruvian shamanism and were mesa carriers in the high Andes tradition. I had some very interesting experiences, but what stood out clearly to me was that I was drawn to the animals more than the sacred sites. Indeed, I had only come on the trip because the second half was a trip to the Peruvian jungle. My classmates were excited about the opportunity to experience ayahuasca, something I had no intention of trying. I wanted to see the jungle and all the animals I was sure must live there.

But before I could experience the jungle, we had many places to visit in the Cusco area. One of the things that I noticed was the lack of domestic animals like cats and dogs. Outside of a major city like Lima, the culture was still very agriculturally based, and with a low-income level, few people owned pets. I saw a lot of llamas, alpacas, donkeys, and guinea pigs, which are farmed like our chickens here.

As a result, I raised more than a few eyebrows in a restaurant one night when I insisted on sharing half my dinner with a cat who had crept out to watch the people eat. I was just so happy to see him that I felt I had to share the joy.

Of all the sites in the Sacred Valley, the most famous is Machu Picchu. I must confess that because I knew so many mesa carriers, I had looked at many photos of Machu Picchu over the years and was expecting to be underwhelmed. I was wrong.

Our arrival at Machu Picchu was shamanically blessed since country-wide Peru was about to shut down completely due to a worker's strike. We even saw the military with guns at transportation points. Somehow, our guide managed to get us onto the last train to Machu Picchu. Usually, Machu Picchu is crowded with tourists. This time, other than the few people already staying there or those hiking in via the Inca Trail, we would have Machu Picchu to ourselves.

We got up so early that the mountains were completely shrouded in mist. It was looking like it might be a very grey and gloomy day. A gentle breeze swirled the mist, and now and again, you would catch a tantalizing glimpse of the mountains and Machu Picchu.

Slowly, the mist lifted, and the sun emerged. And there, spread out below us, was the ancient, mystical city of Machu Picchu. The vivid green grass of each terrace was outlined by the silvery gray of the Stone People, who were arranged into steps, walls, and plazas, looking as if they had emerged from the mountain itself. It was breathtaking.

When we descended to the city itself, we were greeted by a Mama Llama calling for her strayed baby. She was very patient with our frenzy of cameras.

Mama Llama at Machu Picchu.

Llamas are native to Peru. Meeting my first free-roaming one was a big moment personally and spiritually. I have always had a fondness for them, and they are considered sacred in the Peruvian shamanic tradition. The lives of the mountain people and the llamas are intertwined. The villagers create beautifully woven textiles from their wool for clothing, ceremonial cloths, and gorgeous decorations for the llamas. I am particularly fond of how the woven ear tassels look and how the llamas show off a bit with their noses in the air.

Machu Picchu had a herd of llamas and alpacas living on site. Their grazing helped keep the grass in check, and of course, they looked quite stunning.

In the late afternoon, my friend Elaine and I found a gorgeous place to rest. Amazingly, we had a whole section of Machu Picchu to ourselves.

I chose a large rock outcropping overlooking the great city. The sun had warmed the rock perfectly, and I snuggled down into the stone like a satisfied feline. All around me, the stunningly beautiful native fuschia were in full bloom, and I could hear the rhythmic tick-tick sounds of hummingbirds busily feeding on their nectar.

Elaine sat on the ground below my rocky outcropping and opened up her mesa to create sacred space, a magical space between the worlds where Spirit and consensual reality meet. Taking out her flute, she began to play, creating the melody as she went along, inspired by the beauty around her. Her music, the hummingbirds' sounds, and the stone's warmth lulled me into deeper drowsiness, but suddenly, my other senses nudged me into wakefulness—something was different. I heard birds singing, and they sounded very close.

Glancing down, I saw a small flock of birds arrayed in a half circle in front of Elaine and her open mesa. They were so close she could have touched them. The birds reveled in the shamanic energy and added their voices to her melody in celebration.

The author at the Pachamama Stone, Machu Picchu.

THE LLAMA AND THE DEATH RITES

Many scholars have speculated, but no one knows the real purpose of Machu Picchu and its role in the lives of the Inka people. There is a flat stone with steps leading up to it that is said to be the Death Stone, where it was believed that medicine people would undergo a rite of passage.

Our group leader had gotten permission for us to enter Machu Picchu at night, which is no longer allowed. There, we would undergo the Death Rites, which are reputed to allow us to step beyond the death that had been stalking us and create a new reality.

Reentering Machu Picchu at night, with all the Star Brothers and Sisters above us, was incredibly powerful and humbling. There was no one else there but our group, the wildlife, and the spirits whose presence I could feel.

We split into two groups, and I chose to go to the Main Temple Plaza, where earlier that day, I had seen a native Chinchilla cheekily peeking at me from one of the temple niches.

Chinchilla hiding in temple niche.

Shamanic teacher Mary Blankenship was in charge of our group and shared the process with us. We would each lie down upon the stone, and with the help of an assistant, she would extract our spirits from our bodies and toss them to Choquichinchay, the archetypal jaguar in the Peruvian shamanic tradition.

Choquichinchay would swallow our spirit and take it on a journey through the universe. When she spit us back out, our spirits would be cleansed of the old markers of death, offering the opportunity for a conscious death, and the shaman (in this case, Mary) would place our cleansed spirits back in our bodies.

I have always felt a special connection to Choquichinchay, the Rainbow Jaguar who stands with a foot in each world and teaches us to walk with impeccability, grace, and courage. However, I could not help remarking out loud that the "swallowing us up and spitting us out" sounded very much like a shamanic hairball. I'd like to think that my attempt at humor was well received—at least, it amused me.

Overlooking the area of the Main Temple Plaza (lower right).

As an assistant, I was instructed in my duties. Then we began the rite, and I became aware that this was very real. I could feel the weight of each spirit as it was lifted from the body and sense its return to Mary's arms and reunion with the body that was its vessel. It was a profoundly moving experience.

There was just enough light to make out the shapes of the temples around us; there were deep pools of shadows at the base of the walls. Unexpectedly, from the right, a white shape walked toward us. It was one of the male llamas, drawn by the energy and curious about what we were doing,

His timing was less than ideal; he crossed in front of us just as Mary was tossing the spirit of the current person on the death stone up to Choquichinchay, and the spirit sailed right past the llama's ear. If I had needed proof (beyond what my senses had been telling me) that this was real, I received it at that moment.

Spooked by having a spirit tossed through his energy field, the llama leaped forward and crashed into the pile of backpacks our group had left by the base of the wall. As the llama fought to disentangle himself, I braced myself for possibly intervening before the llama or someone else got hurt. Thankfully, the llama righted himself; unharmed, he made a speedy exit.

Eventually, it was my turn to lie down upon the stone, and I admit I had some trepidation. What would this feel like?

I felt my spirit lift out of my body, and I was aware of being in two places at once without a strong awareness of either one. I felt my spirit traveling, and then I heard Mary chuckle. What was that all about? Time passed, and then Mary laughed, something I had definitely not heard when assisting the other participants.

When my spirit was returned to my body, I felt whole again and asked Mary about her laughter.

She told me that when my spirit went out to meet with Choquichinchay, there was a great booming peal of laughter from us both, and she couldn't help but chuckle. Then she said when my spirit returned from its journey, it pounced on her like a cat would and laughed at her surprise. Mary noted my spirit had some weight to it, and she couldn't help but laugh in return. Perhaps there is more to my logo than meets the eye...

After the Death Rites, it was suggested we find a place to sit quietly in meditation. Somehow, I ended up by myself on a side of Machu Picchu that none of the other practitioners had chosen. But I was not alone. The herd of llamas and alpacas grazed and rested nearby.

Striding through the ruins, a huge elemental spirit passed us by, and I wondered just how much I missed seeing in those places between the worlds.

In the silence of the night, I felt an incredible sense of peace and a perfect feeling of rightness in sharing this moment with the native animals. Machu Picchu was so much more than a place of ancient beauty; it was also a place of natural mystery.

TASTES LIKE CHICKEN

When preparing what we needed to pack for our trip to the Sacred Valley and the jungle, we were told we would be doing something quintessentially Peruvian—visiting a restaurant that prepares and serves roast guinea pig.

I've known several guinea pigs, but only as pets, not as food. As a child, my sister had one named Beth who would emit ear-splitting shrieks when she wanted something special to eat, which happened frequently. Beth had quite the repertoire of other conversational sounds; the one that sounded like a churring version of a purr was one of my favorites.

However, in Peru, guinea pigs are a native species raised as food in rural homes—much as we raise chickens here.

I believe that when one is a guest in a foreign country, one should respect cultural differences. So, for this challenging dining experience, I decided to put on my game face in the form of a t-shirt that I packed special for the occasion.

The t-shirt showed a Kliban cat holding a mouse up by its tail, accompanied by heartfelt words of friendship, "If I had two dead mice, I would give you one." I figured that if I wore that shirt, all I needed to do when presented with a dinner of roast guinea pig would be to shapeshift into my feline power animal, and the rest would take care of itself.

The momentous day arrived, and there was consternation among members of our group—vegetarian and non-vegetarian. T-shirt-wearing and already partly shifted into feline mode, my power animal could not understand what all the fuss was about. This was simply another form of sustenance to him.

I found myself in the unusual position of bringing messages from the animals to two men who were the most freaked out and coaching them through how to deal with this from a shamanic perspective.

We arrived at the restaurant devoted solely to preparing slow-roasted guinea pigs in special clay ovens. It sounded like quite the production, and we were assured that Peruvians consider it a very special occasion. Now, the pressure was definitely on to *not* be the rude American.

After we had enjoyed some appetizers and perhaps more libations than usual, the star of the hour appeared. Our roast guinea pig arrived splendidly arrayed on a platter carried by a proud serving person, and we all gaped with amazement. It was a whole guinea pig with a fruit in its mouth. It looked startlingly like a medieval–style roast pig in miniature.

Once we all had a chance to admire the artistry and salivate over the deliciousness to come, the roast guinea pig was returned to the kitchen, where we were assured it would be carved up along with others and returned for our dining delight.

I looked over at my two shamanic protégées, and they weren't green, so I took that as a good sign.

Eventually, portions of roast guinea pig arrived at our table, and the serving dish was passed from person to person so that each could select their part of choice. I was aware of some consternation but did not realize precisely why until the dish was placed before me. Yes, the guinea pig had been carved into the equivalent of small versions of leg and thigh, but with one big difference—each drumstick ended in a paw!

I took a deep breath and shifted fully into my feline power animal. From that place of connection with the natural world, I grasped the leg with a sense of amusement that it could grasp me back rather than one of horror and took my first bite. Despite the paw, my power animal and I agreed that guinea pig tastes like chicken.

JUNGLE BOOGIE

Our journey to the Amazon jungle involved a ride on the Amazon River in what looked like a larger version of a dugout canoe with a canopy and motor. As we putted along, I wondered what kinds of fish we were passing over and desperately hoped for a wildlife sighting —a jaguar would be ideal, of course!

For months before I left for this trip, I had daydreamed about seeing a jaguar in his jungle habitat. In my fantasy, the jaguar behaved more like a large domestic cat rather than the huge predator he truly was. Maybe there would be some Reiki involved...

I enjoyed my boat trip on the Amazon, although there were fewer birds than I had expected, and I saw no wildlife, perhaps because the river was wide and we were not close to shore.

However, a lovely surprise awaited us when we arrived at the Biological Reserve, our home for the next week. As we disembarked, our biologist host and staff handed us tropical fruit drinks, including straws. I felt like I had dropped into a scene from *Fantasy Island*, with one major exception—we were also greeted by five peccaries—wild jungle pigs. We were told that the people who lived at the station rescued them as orphans and raised them like pets.

I was delighted to meet them, but some group members were less so. The peccaries were social and believed in mingling with the humans. One was a full-grown boar, meaning he had tusks, a little attitude, and a lot of smell.

Wild peccary greets our group at landing.

I watched the boar target one woman who looked particularly out of place in the jungle in how she was dressed. The boar moved in close. The woman was decidedly not thrilled about all the attention she was getting, so she put her drink down on the bench, stood up, and moved away from him, which was exactly what the boar had planned. Moving in, he knocked over the sweet tropical drink that had been his real focus and began lapping it up with great grunts of enjoyment.

I laughed silently at his cleverness and made friends with the peccaries, petting them (including the wily boar) and telling them how charming they were.

The smallest of the peccaries was named Juanita, and she was still a youngster. We hit it off for some reason, and for my entire stay she would seek me out or respond when I called her. She often walked with me and did an amazing job of voluntarily heeling on my left side, just as if I had taught her to do so. None of my dogs were ever as good at heeling as Juanita was!

One night, as we were companionably walking back to my hut after dinner, Juanita demonstrated just how smart she truly was. She was in her usual position on my left side, but we were not in synch speed-wise. She ended up several feet ahead of me, and instead of waiting for me to catch up, she backed up in a straight line until she was once again even with me. Then, we continued on our walk as a matched pair.

I made friends with several other animals/birds that lived there, but the one (besides Juanita) who stands out in my memory is the camp tomcat. He was a handsome orange tiger only about a year old, and they mostly kept him to help keep the rodent population in check.

When we first met, I was so happy to see a friendly cat face that I swamped him with affection, which he adored. I told him which hut I was staying in, gave him specific directions, and told him he was welcome any time. Each hut was raised off the ground for safety's sake, so there were stairs to our door. He often napped on our steps for the rest of my stay. We left the door open at night so he could come and go as he pleased.

The camp cat snoozing on our stairs.

One moonlit night, the camp cat came by for a visit. He jumped up on the bed I was lying in and trilled at me. He looked deep into my eyes and held eye contact. I felt myself falling into their depths. I felt wrapped in affection. His purr was deeply resonant music, and as he slowly sashayed up the bed, I realized, to my amazement, that he was courting me! What next ensued was hilarious, and my roommate slept through it all.

Like some maiden out of a dime novel I made protestations of being the wrong species—we were incompatible. Not wanting him to feel rejected, I assured him that no human male had ever sung so sweetly or showered me with such loving affection, but we could only be friends. He continued his pursuit up the bed, and I finally had to climb out of it before things got out of hand. Poor guy, it was lonely in the jungle, and apparently, I was the first to come along that truly appreciated him...but sadly, it was not to be.

CROCODILE REIKI

Out of all the guest huts, ours was situated closest to the jungle. Every morning, I awoke to the sound of the jungle birds greeting the day. The most memorable was one I called the Raindrop Bird since his call sounded just like a melodious raindrop splashing into a pool of water.

A trail led into the jungle near the steps of our hut, and following it took you to the fenced area where the biologists kept young crocodiles in a watery pen. The local jaguars had decimated the younger crocodile population, leaving the larger, older, and more dangerous crocs alone. Without intervention, the entire population would disappear since there would be no up-and-coming generations to replace the older ones as they aged and died. So, the biologists captured the younger crocs, brought them to this holding area for a few years until they grew large enough to be less at risk, and then returned them to the wild.

You could walk through the fenced area on planks suspended above the water. Of course, we were given all kinds of instructions on what not to do, but that was more to protect the crocodiles than us since they were very shy. All I ever saw of them while in there were the occasional pair of eyes peeking up from the water.

One day, I went by myself to see if I could glimpse one on land. Instead of going in, I began walking around the fencing outside to see if any crocodiles had hauled out to sun themselves.

Crocodile sunning in a patch of sunlight.

As I rounded the corner, I saw what appeared to be one of the larger crocodiles basking in the corner down at the end. Mindful of how shy the wild crocs had been, immediately sliding into the water when we tried to approach by boat, I stopped and reached out to him mentally and energetically. I introduced myself and asked if he would like some Reiki. He was receptive, so I began sending Reiki as I slowly walked along the fence in his direction. When I was about eight feet away, I felt as though I had reached a boundary line—any closer and he would run away—so I stopped, and we simply communed for a while in the energy.

JAGUAR COMES A-CALLIN'

One moonlit night, not long after the camp cat came a-courtin', I was awakened by the hair-raising sound of the peccaries loudly squealing and gnashing their teeth in alarm while running for their lives. They emerged from the jungle and ran right past our hut.

I rolled over and looked at the clock—it was 4 a.m. The rest of the camp was silent—all the other people (and my roommate) were still asleep. I idly wondered what had alarmed the peccaries so much, and since I was semi-awake, I decided to make a trip to the bathroom.

Our jungle hut bathroom was very airy; instead of a door, it had a bamboo curtain. As I was exiting the bathroom, my body suddenly stopped moving forward. All the hairs on the back of my neck stood up. I could feel a presence outside the hut, an energy that the DNA of my ancient ancestors recognized on a primal level.

Although I could neither see nor hear a thing from where I was standing, I *knew* there was a jaguar right outside our hut. Almost simultaneously, I remembered we had left the hut door open per usual to allow the camp cat to come and go; there was no barrier between the jaguar and me.

One part of my brain thought it was hilarious that I would think for a moment that a flimsy screen door would stop the jaguar if he wanted to drop in for a visit.

Another part of my brain desperately wanted my body to move so I could see the jaguar. I tried to move in that direction and discovered that I literally couldn't—my guides were preventing me from doing so. If I thought about moving to the bed, I could move. If I thought about moving to the door, I couldn't. Frustrated, I argued with them, but they were having none of it: I was to go back to bed and stay there, so that is what I ended up doing.

I mentioned the incident later at breakfast. Apparently, I was the only one who heard the alarm calls of my peccary friends, and everyone was prepared to write my story off as an overactive imagination since I was assured that it is unusual for wild jaguars to come near people. However, the camp biologist looked and found the pugmark of a male jaguar right outside our hut.

The jaguar had come a-callin'.

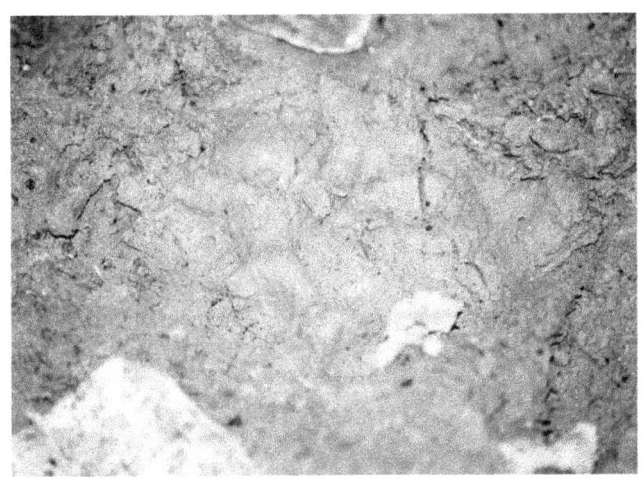

Jungle Jaguar's pawprint

COLLEGE LIFE AND RESCUE WORK

Storytelling #4

UNDER HER PAW

Growing up with a mother who was animal crazy, my father, sisters, and I were surrounded by animals of all species. We always had dogs and cats, but there were times when we had canaries, a chicken, a variety of fish and amphibians, and a revolving door for rescued baby bunnies, starlings, wild ducklings, and essentially anyone else who seemed in need of support.

When I left South Jersey at 17 to go to college in Massachusetts, it surprised me to discover that the adjustment I struggled with was not homesickness but animal contact withdrawal.

The first two weeks were challenging. I had to cope not only with adjusting to college life with new schedules, new friends, and terrible food but also with life without *any* animals at all. I had not realized that it would be possible to live without their loving support—they had always been a part of my world, and I was completely unprepared for how lonely I was without them. I think my roommate was struggling with it a bit, too. Living in the college dorm, we were forbidden to have pets, but one day, I came back to our room to discover that my roommate had rescued some mice from the lab where she was studying biology. They were a very nice surprise, indeed.

Our room was on the third floor, overlooking a school with an asphalt-paved yard. The only greenery was a beautiful maple tree dressed in its fall colors. Its beauty offered me some comfort in the midst of my major lifestyle adjustment.

The universe apparently agreed that life without animals was a highly unnatural way for me to live, and one day, I found myself taken under the guiding paw of one of the campus dogs. Her name was Samantha, and her markings and overall appearance reminded me a bit of my mother's dog Lady Jane. Samantha also had a bit of Lady Jane's loyalty since I would frequently find her lying on the hallway floor outside the door to my room, waiting for me to return.

Samantha and Rose in dorm room.

At that time it was the custom for students to bring their dogs to campus to roam for the day while they were in class, and many of the local residents also allowed their dogs to roam freely. As a result, there were usually packs of dogs hanging out wherever you went. I don't recall how or when I first met Samantha, but she was well known on the campus, which is how I learned her name and that she had a home to go to at night.

Samantha had student life down pat. Once she had adopted me, I would find her patiently waiting outside the door of my room when I returned from classes. To do this, she would first have to wait for another student to buzz her in through the locked dormitory access door. Then, she would climb the stairs to the third floor where I lived. I was told that while she was friendly to those who said "hi" to her, she was on a mission to see me.

I have no idea what I did to earn her friendship other than the fact that I needed her company, and I paid attention to her. Since she had a home, I never fed her or bought her a toy. Looking back, I don't think I even had a water bowl for her. And yet she would stay by my side for whatever activity I was engaged in.

One memorable day, I decided that I was going to walk downtown by myself for the first time. Now, you have to understand that this was a big deal since, at the time, Clark University was surrounded by what used to be a blue-collar neighborhood that had fallen on hard times. At our student orientation, we were told to *never* walk the streets around the campus alone, especially at night, as we would be in danger. Having seen inner city Philadelphia first hand, I thought they were going a bit overboard, and of course, ignored their advice.

On my way to Main Street, Samantha found me and decided to accompany me. That was when I discovered that Samantha had one highly unusual and somewhat embarrassing habit—she would grab a passing stranger by the leg and proceed to hump it. At that moment, I did everything I could to pretend she was *not* with me! There wasn't much I could have done since I never had her on a leash. At all times, it was her choice to stay with me. I don't know if it was her intention, but I turned back to the college since I did not want her to follow me too far from the neighborhood she was familiar with.

As time went by, I settled more into college life and even acquired a boyfriend who happened to live on the second floor of my dorm. As I began spending more time in his room, Samantha's routine changed to checking my room first and then his. By this time, it was an accepted fact that she was *my* dog, and students would direct her to where they had last seen me.

I used to talk to Samantha quite a bit. She definitely helped ease my loneliness. She would keep me company while I studied, patiently sitting or lying on the floor or my bed.

Occasionally, she would distract me by focusing her attention on one spot on the wall. She would watch that spot with great intensity—so focused that I would have to get up and see if she was watching a spider, but there was never anything that I could see. What she would do next would truly unnerve me. Her gaze would move from that spot, her head turning slowly, eyes moving across the wall—she was tracking something intently, but what? Eventually, it would be too much for me—it was simply too unnerving. Spooked, I'd leave off studying, and we'd go out for a walk—she made me feel like invisible spirits were in the room with us. I'll never know for sure whether she truly saw spirit beings or whether Samantha had come up with a truly stellar way to get me outside where we could have some fun together.

I always left it up to Samantha to decide when she wanted to go home to her other life. As time went by, she spent more and more time with me, even spending the night a few times.

One day, she didn't appear as usual. Days went by, and still no Samantha. I asked around, and the general rumor was that her people got tired of her not being around and started keeping her in. Someone else said they moved. We did not get to say goodbye; I never saw her again.

Samantha, wherever you are now, thank you for choosing to love and support me through a difficult time and reminding me that the animals always walk with me.

PARTY CAT

Dorm life got progressively more interesting as my fellow students and I became more comfortable with our new lives away from home and our parents. We began to fully explore all the opportunities to be young, have fun, and make our own mistakes.

One of my new friends was a year or two ahead and living off-campus. She had a cat that had just had a litter of kittens; they were all polydactyls. Some had more toes than others, and I was particularly fond of the classic tabby male who looked like he had baseball mitts for paws.

The inevitable happened. There was one other person in our entire dorm with an older kitten, and so far, the DAs—who were supposed to keep us in line—were turning a blind eye. So, I adopted him against the rules and with no visible means of support other than the benevolence of my family, who were underwriting my education. My roommate and I were now living with mice, a kitten, and occasionally Samantha, the dog. From my perspective, life was now much more normal, even if we were all crammed together in a small room.

However, rather like the rest of the students in the dorm, we did not all stay in our little boxes. It was 1976, the tail end of the cultural revolution of the 60s. Our dorm was progressive: the first floor and the third floor were female only, and the second floor was male only. Over time, couples paired off, and living arrangements shifted dramatically. All bathrooms became co-ed, something we were sure would have horrified our parents, and of course, that made it even more wickedly, deliciously fun.

And my newly named kitten Marquis was part of all the craziness. It turned out that he was *very* social. He loved roaming the halls and visiting with whoever was having the most fun. If I wanted to find him, I only had to go where there was the most noise. He even enjoyed an occasional skateboard ride. As he got older, I would discover that he had left the building via an open first-floor window and was happily sunning himself on the lawn alongside his vastly expanded student family.

Marquis lounges in a bean bag chair.

Marquis adopted some of our bad habits, too—he liked to smoke pot. And when he was high, he got the munchies and would happily join us in eating whatever snacks we were having. From my vantage point now, I shudder to think about some of the things he actually consumed. It is a wonder he survived kittenhood with my less-than-stellar care of him. Thankfully, he thrived.

He became a legend in the dorm for playing tag. If you tagged him and ran away, he would run after you, tag you, turn and run, and repeat...

Marquis also enjoyed driving my not-as-animal-friendly boyfriend crazy by taking over the fishnet suspended from the ceiling of his dorm room, which he shared with his best friend, who was dating my best friend.

My boyfriend had strung the fishing net with colored Christmas lights, and they looked very pretty at night when we would listen to rock music on the stereo. We never did manage to discover how Marquis got up there, but it became his personal kitty hammock—a habit that we could never get him to quit.

Indeed, he'd have a wicked gleam in his eyes when we found him up there. Marquis did enjoy winding my boyfriend up just a little bit...but isn't that what cat friends are for?

ANIMAL HEALERS: THE CATS OF KITTY HARBOR

I recently resumed volunteering at Kitty Harbor, an adoption facility on Harbor Avenue in West Seattle. I'd begun volunteering my animal communication and energy healing services in November, about two weeks before my cat Shaman was diagnosed with terminal cancer.

With Shaman's hospice care and subsequent transition into spirit in late February, I had neither the energy, the time, or the heart to work with the shelter cats. Since his passing, I struggled with deep feelings of loss and grief, the intensity of which alerted me that I was dealing with some old issues, not just normal grief around his death. Many healing sessions for myself resulted, and while I experienced major clearings, I did wonder how I would feel returning to work with the shelter cats. Would seeing a black-and-white kitten or cat cause me to tear up?

My worries were temporarily laid to rest when I arrived at the shelter by being submerged in the overwhelming number of cats and kittens in need.

My first client was a grief-stricken, scared Mama cat who had not eaten in days and was uncomfortable from her spay surgery. Her kittens had been taken from her so that they could be socialized to be good people companions, a necessary measure since her motherly efforts to protect her kittens by attacking the volunteers were sending the kittens the wrong message. With kittens, there is about a six- to eight-week period after birth where they can imprint on humans and become good companions. Otherwise, they can become feral, like this cat Mama.

But the mother cat knew none of this; all she knew when I talked with her was that she had been unable to protect her kittens enough; now they were gone, and she had no reason to go on. I did not just hear her pain; I felt it. Her emotions hit a raw place inside me, and tears began streaming down my face. I let her feel my pain on her behalf and then began to gently ease hers energetically while explaining what had happened and why; her kittens were being cared for and would ultimately have homes where there would be enough food, they would never know cold, or be chilled by rain. I explained that they would live much longer than any cat living rough as a feral, and hopefully, they would know love.

She heard me, taking the information in, but it comforted her little. I acknowledged that she needed to go through a grieving process, such as I was, and that only time could heal her loss. I told her I would do what I could to rebalance her energetically but that it would be up to her to find a reason to go on living —that I could not help her with. I reassured her that Delyn, the founder of Kitty Harbor, had a place in the country lined up where she could be free, take shelter in a barn when she wished, hunt as she liked, and avoid the people she feared.

The heartbroken mother only asked one thing of me: that the Reiki attunement I offered her also be given to her kittens. I agreed willingly. I said I would do the attunement for the entire family simultaneously so they could be together again, if only in the energy. She accepted, and when I completed the process for all, I wished her well and moved on to those next in need.

Kitty Harbor has two main sections: one where cats and kittens are available for adoption and the other for those who are sick and need to be isolated and cared for.

Many patients were in the sick ward that day—there wasn't a single empty cage.

One kitten had a mysterious illness; I could see red ulcers in his mouth, preventing him from eating well. Despite feeling horrible, he looked at me and smiled (this is an interpretation of his communication), and my heart reached out to him. I hope my attitude is as good as his if I ever feel that ill.

Seeing how many sick cats needed attention, I realized that while I could offer special attention to a few, I would need to do some group work for all to benefit.

Next, I headed toward the open area, where many adult cats and kittens roam freely. It is a cat paradise, with scratching posts, tunnels, cool hiding places, and open spaces to run and play. The downside is that Kitty Harbor is in a busy area, right by the exit for the West Seattle Bridge and next to the train tracks. Sometimes, the sound and vibration are deafening, but few cats or kittens allow it to disturb their routines.

I had been carrying my open mesa in a wicker basket. The basket enables me to be mobile from room to room and keeps the mesa clean. I learned the hard way not to place my open mesa directly on the floor; not only do some of the kittens try to steal my shamanic items, but they also track kitty litter through it!

Mobile mesa and I entered the open area. Tigger, an eight-year-old orange and white tiger cat, immediately rushed up to me.

Tigger greets Rose with intensity.

Tigger took one look into the basket and wanted that shamanic energy bad. Holding him back from rooting around in my mesa, I chose the carved stone I think of as my Unconditional Love stone, the one gifted to me by cat Gracie after her passing. Extending my hand holding the Stone Person toward Tigger so that he could sniff, instead, he made me laugh by grabbing my wrist, pulling the stone to his face, and alternating licking with trying to chew the carvings off it. He wanted to eat the energy!

He was licking the stone so furiously that a passing volunteer wanted to know what was on it. Deciding that chewing on the Stone Person was still not close enough to the energy, Tigger stuffed my fingers into his mouth and tried to chew the energy off them! Fortunately, he was gentle, but I could still feel the sharpness of his teeth.

Prying Tigger off my hand, I distracted him by placing the mesa stone on the ground. Next, I offered him a Reiki attunement, figuring that if there was ever a cat in love with energy, it was Tigger. He gratefully accepted the attunement, blissfully clutching my mesa stone to his chest and licking it the entire time. By the time the attunement was complete, Tigger had calmed down, and I could place the Stone Person back in the basket. Tigger then settled in front of the basket, repelling other cats wanting to check out *his* mesa, and relaxed into basking in its energy glow. I could now turn my attention to the other cats patiently waiting their turn.

Sitting on the floor, I invited any who wanted to come closer. Most volunteers at Kitty Harbor must spend their time cleaning litter boxes and feeding the cats and kittens. It takes one person about two hours to take care of them, so the cats highly value the opportunity for personal interaction.

Tortie kitten Witchy Woman shares a few requests.

First to approach was a tortie kitten who climbed into my lap, sat down, and stared directly into my eyes without blinking (very un-catlike behavior). From this tiny scrap of skinny kitten, I got a sense of timelessness, a definite understanding of energy, and past lives of working with it! When I gently stroked her with a finger, she began to purr but did none of the everyday kitten things—she was content to sit in the energy while I worked with the other cats. I nicknamed her Witchy Woman; she would make some energy person a fine companion.

Off to the side was the dreaded black-and-white kitten I had feared encountering. Skinny as a rail, the kitten's body type reminded me a lot of Shaman. Rescued from terrible situations, many of these kittens require good nutrition and medical attention, which they receive as soon as they arrive, but it takes a little while for them to get some meat on their bones.

The black-and-white kitten was hanging back, close enough to be in my energy field but not wanting to intrude on my interlude with Witchy Woman. I nicknamed him Tuxedo Guy.

Reaching out to pick him up, I sensed a slight timidity and a hint of feeling unloved. Pushing my personal feelings aside, I placed him on my leg and opened my heart and the energy to him. I now had a purring kitten perched on either leg, and Tigger was still doing his repelling-all-mesa-boarders act in front of me. We were quite a sight!

Tigger did not prevent the rest of the cats from coming over to me; one at a time, they detoured around him—joining the two kittens; neither Witchy Woman nor Tuxedo Guy minded sharing.

Opening my senses wider, I began to look for what was needed. I got more than I bargained for—all of the cats were wide open in the combination of shamanic and Reiki energy, and through them, I connected to cats beyond Kitty Harbor, including ferals and street cats.

This part is challenging to put into words because it came all at once in a jumble. I was flooded with feelings of happiness from the cats at Kitty Harbor; they were safe, dry, cared for, loved, and well-fed. They lived in the moment, aware that they could cease to exist at any time, for such was life, which was okay. No matter what they had been through before being rescued, what mattered was now and the energy.

I understood I was now connecting on another level beyond this pacha (time/place). For lack of a better word, I sensed the presence of cat goddess Bast and felt overwhelmed. I had to pull back; it was too much, my human heart could not take it all in. I felt hopeless in the face of so many cats and other animals in need. With a sinking feeling, I knew I still had much more work to do around my loss and attachment issues, for the cats had no such feelings; this was my battle.

Feeling humbled, I decided that the best way to honor what I had experienced was to offer a group Reiki attunement to all the cats and kittens at Kitty Harbor. The purpose of the group attunement is to assist each in connecting to the universal life force energy or Reiki for the highest and greatest good for that particular individual, mentally, emotionally, physically, and spiritually (especially spiritually after what I had just experienced). When we finished, Delyn would be surrounded by 150 Reiki cats!

Making sure I was very grounded, I reached out with my awareness to all the cats in the facility. Beginning the attunement process, I invited each to participate, acknowledging that some might not wish to and accepting their right to choose. During the attunement, activity slowed where I was and became much quieter. A sense of timelessness enveloped the area. When the attunement was complete, many cats opted to take naps, feeling quite relaxed. I felt a bit tired. I had just had my consciousness raised, and my energy vastly expanded!

Tigger was now very calm, and I had no trouble packing up my mesa. With difficulty, I said goodbye to Witchy Woman and Tuxedo Guy. I was sorely tempted to inquire about adopting Witchy Woman but felt in my heart that it was not her path to come and live with me; once again, this was my issue.

As I said farewell to my many new cat friends, I sincerely hoped each would find the loving home they so richly deserved. I trusted that I had done all I could that day to assist each cat in their journey; I knew they had done all they could to teach me about mine. Despite my sadness, I knew I would return; there was much wisdom to learn from the cats of Kitty Harbor.[*]

---

[*] *Since my visit, Kitty Harbor has morphed into Emerald City Kitty Harbor to better serve the cats and kittens of the Seattle area. Please take a moment to visit their website, donate, or consider volunteering or fostering where you live.*

TRAVELS WITH ROSE

Storytelling #5

A STORY FOR AFRICAN GREY PARROT MAX

In my efforts to offer as many Zoo Animal Ambassadors as possible the opportunity to participate in shamanic ceremonies and to connect with them and listen, I make unofficial visits to a few local places regularly. I aim to visit at least once a year, but sometimes, that just doesn't work out.

I revisited Cougar Mountain Zoo a few months ago [2015] and discovered a lot more time than a year had passed since I had been there. The three mountain lion cubs had grown into gorgeous and personable adults—one of whom I feel may grow into an important teacher. Time will tell.

Cougar Mountain had just gotten four very young male wolf pups, who were adorable. They feel like a counterpoint to the four female wolves at the Woodland Park Zoo. I look forward to seeing how that plays out in ceremonies.

Most startling (in a good way) was Cougar Mountain's new Bird World, a brand-new area with lovely toys and other amenities just for parrots, macaws, and cockatoos.

When I first walked in, I was awestruck by its magnificence and unsure whom to approach first. As I walked down the line and said hello to each bird, I felt pulled toward an African Grey parrot named Max.

When I stopped in front of Max he gave me a look that said he was interested, but I felt he was reserving judgment—I had to prove myself. I have absolutely no idea what prompted me to do this (Spirit, most likely), but I said aloud to Max, "I want to tell you a story." And I proceeded to tell him about a recent event concerning my cat—one I have tentatively entitled "Manitou and the Hummingbird." It is a story I have not yet written down, so Max got to hear it first. [Note: I never did write it down, so Max had a special performance.]

The whole time I was telling him this story, one part of my brain was saying to me, "Seriously? You tell a bird a story about a cat?" However, another part of me felt strongly that Max would really enjoy the conclusion.

Rose tells a story to African Grey Max.

I told the story with a combination of spoken words and mental images. Max was a quiet but attentive audience. I finished, and if I was expecting parrot applause I didn't get it. I did feel as though I had passed some sort of test, although I have no idea what the criteria were. I bowed to Max, thanked him for listening, and moved on.

I returned a month or so later, and when I said hello to Max, he mentally asked me if I had another story. I smiled at him, and to verify that I had understood correctly, I verbally asked, "You'd like another story?"

I expected Max to reply mentally. Instead—OUT LOUD—he said very clearly, "Yes."

I was floored. I am used to animals responding mentally. I've never had one reply back verbally in English since most species simply can't. I felt deeply honored that Max chose to do that since he had never made a sound before that moment.

I laughed with delight and said, "It's a doozy," (referring to the story). Then, I proceeded to tell Max all about how the Orcas responded when we showed up in answer to their call for event *Whale Teachers #2: The Orcas* and all of the incredible, amazing things that happened during the long time they spent with us.

Max seemed to enjoy the story—he never took his eyes off me. I sensed his excitement about the events and that he was glad to hear something interesting rather than the usual way we talk to parrots.

Maybe next time, I'll ask Max what kind of story he wants to hear. Who knows what he'll say?

Postscript from 2017: I visited Cougar Mountain Zoo earlier this year, but it was too cold for the parrots to be outside. I asked one of the keepers about Max, and she said he was doing well. He recovered from his respiratory illness, but because of scarring, he could only go out when the weather was warm enough. So I told her how Max liked stories and what he said to me, and she told me he was really smart; so smart it is almost scary. She shared that one day, while she was leaning down to clean up the floor in their open area, Max moved down the pole so that he was close to her ear and whispered, "Help us."

HITTING THE ROAD IN A '63 CHEVY

arty cat Marquis came into my life during my freshman year in college in 1976, and he livened up life for all the residents of the three floors of the dormitory. But all parties end sometime, and as summer approached, I knew I needed to make a decision about what to do with Marquis while my boyfriend and I embarked on the six-week cross-country trip we had been planning for the majority of the school year.

We had saved up as much money as we possibly could, but we would be car camping, staying at free or low-cost camp-grounds as we headed for the mecca of the California coast, at least 3000 miles from Massachusetts. This was not a trip to take Marquis on, especially since he had little experience with car travel, and it was unlikely in the extreme that my boyfriend would have embraced the idea.

So, I came up with a plan that I thought might suit. I resolved to throw myself on the mercy of my grandmother and great-aunt in New Jersey. The outcome was by no means certain. As a child, I spent time with my Nana and Aunt Tot's Dalmatian dog Candy, but she had crossed over many years ago. She was buried in the Clara Glenn pet cemetery located a block from their house, and we frequently visited her grave, so I knew that she held an important place in their hearts, but in all the years since, they had not adopted another dog.

Despite our family having some, I had no idea where my grandmother and aunt stood regarding cats. I hoped that as firstborn grandchild, I would hold a special place in their hearts, and when I asked—thankfully—they were willing.

My father was definitely not supportive of the cross-country trip (and perhaps my boyfriend). As I said to my father (perhaps prophetically), when else might I ever have six weeks to just hit the road and explore? He essentially told me I was on my own—if anything happened, he was not paying for it.

So, bravely, Marquis and I set out from Massachusetts in my boyfriend's flat black '63 Chevy Nova that he had rescued for the princely sum of one dollar and lovingly babied long before we had met.

My boyfriend loved that car. He'd installed a state-of-the-art removable 8-track system with speakers in the doors and rear ledge and then installed an alarm system so that he could chase any would-be thieves off if the car were broken into. And the entire dorm actually saw that in action one evening when the alarm went off from down the street. My boyfriend and his best friend instantly grabbed up weapons—one of which happened to be an ax—and went charging down the second-floor stairs and out into the street, yelling like Viking berserkers (which they surely looked like). My best girlfriend and I sat there in total shock—who were these guys, really? It turned out to be a false alarm (of which there were many to come). We were the talk of the dorm for a while.

If the challenge of the car being 14 years old was not enough for our road trip, my boyfriend had also covered the side windows with a film; you could see out from inside the car, but from the outside, the windows was reflective—no one could see in. It looked really cool, but that—and perhaps the fact that we both looked like hippies—got us pulled over by the state troopers on our way to New Jersey to see my family and drop Marquis off at my Nana and Aunt Tot's. We had not even begun our trip, and we were already having adventures—more excitement that Marquis would miss out on. And he missed out on a lot more since highway patrol routinely stopped us throughout the trip. We must have looked like complete burnouts since (more than once) we had cars pull up next to us on the highway at 55 mph, roll down their passenger side window, and ask if we had any weed for sale!

When we finally departed from South Jersey, I was a mixture of equal parts excitement, fear, and sadness. As I waved goodbye to Nana, Aunt Tot, and Marquis, I knew I would miss him and that Marquis' life would now be a *lot* quieter than the dorm where there was always something going on. On the flip side, he would have their undivided attention, and I was confident that Nana and Aunt Tot would spoil him with treats like they did my sisters and me. Being food and affection-oriented, I knew Marquis would enjoy that.

TRAVELS WITH ROSE

Several moments stand out in my memory of our cross-country travels, most of them animal and nature-related.

Due to stops along the way, we often arrived at the free campgrounds after dark. One memorable night, there was a pull-in right by the side of the road that our guidebook said was free, but it did not have signage. Mileage-wise, we thought we were in the right place, but we were simply too tired to care if we weren't.

We pitched the tent, and I cooked dinner in the dark as best I could. We retired shortly thereafter.

A few hours later, there was this terrible scary noise, and I shot bolt upright in fear. It was a train whistle. It was really, really loud and really close. The inside of the tent was lit up like it was broad daylight, and the beam of the headlight was coming straight through the front of the tent. For one heart-stopping moment, I thought we had been so tired when we set up camp that we hadn't noticed we were setting up on the train tracks.

Thankfully, we were just right next to them. There was a reason why the camping area was free...

The next morning provided the perfect humorous counterpoint to my rush of fear the night before. Preparing to greet the day, I opened the tent flap and discovered a herd of cows staring at me. They were all gathered at the fence across the two-lane secondary road. I could tell they were curious about their new neighbors, so I walked across to say hello, but before I could reach them, the entire herd turned tail in unison and ran away. Given that they outnumbered me about 100 to 1, I had to laugh.

Another memory is our arrival at yet another free campground in Kansas. After what seemed like endless amounts of travel across flat prairie with nary a tree in sight in any direction, it was like an oasis to discover several trees at the campsite. Of course, there was a drawback—the toilet facilities were nothing more than a hole in the ground with a handrail to hang on to, but I didn't care since the campground was also the roosting place of a Great Horned Owl! The only time I have seen a wild one.

The faithful Chevy Nova and the joys of car camping.

Another memory is of arriving at a low-cost campground after full dark, later than usual. As we were unpacking, a few Boy Scouts came by and cautioned us to be careful where we set up, as there were fire ants, and they had already killed two rattlesnakes. My boyfriend was terrified of snakes, and as I recall, I was the one who set up most of our camp that night. Thankfully, no one came calling that time.

However, the night we camped in the desert was another story altogether. Since it was a national park, the landscape was pristine, with saguaro cactus raising their arms to the sky everywhere. I had entered the land of Wiley Coyote, and later, we actually had a roadrunner race our car!

I was charmed, and after setting up in the dark for so many nights, it was lovely to enjoy the sunset and the coolness of the desert evening. Until now, my boyfriend and I had been scrupulous about putting all food back into the cooler, cleaning up our cooking equipment, and putting it away so that we did not attract bears or other wildlife. But in that beautiful desert setting, the thought of there being any bears seemed unlikely, so just this once, we decided to forego our usual routine and left our dishes and pots and pans sitting out on the picnic table.

We had been in the tent for about half an hour when we heard the ominous sound of our culinary supplies being moved around. By now, there was a little moonlight, but not a lot, so when I unzipped the tent flap, all I could see were large silhouettes surrounding the picnic table. I had no idea who the shapes belonged to, but they certainly were not human.

I had to know who had come visiting, so I grabbed my shoes (without checking for anyone who might have moved in) and bolted out of the tent. My boyfriend was less curious, and having given up on trying to keep me restrained, he opted to stay in the tent. As a result, he missed out on one of the most beautiful experiences of our trip.

As I got closer, the shapes resolved themselves into a herd of burros. They were delightedly licking the remains of our dinner off the plates, but there was not much left. So, I greeted them respectfully and told them I had some bread.

On my way to get the bread out of the car I excitedly told my boyfriend that it was a wonderful herd of burros, and didn't he want to come out and meet them? Apparently, he did not. So, for the next 10 minutes or so, the burros and I had a party. I passed out slices of bread all around, and the sound of much chewing and lip-smacking broke the silence of the desert. There were 8-10 burros as near as I could tell, and they were very friendly. I scratched, patted, and made much of them to my heart's content. I even hugged one or two. They were so friendly that I figured they must have come from a nearby ranch. I thought about throwing a leg over one and going for a ride. I finally decided that it might not be the proper thing for a host to do to guests, invited or not.

Eventually, I ran out of bread. While the burros seemed happy to have me join their group, a little competition had started over who could be closest to me. Before the hooves and teeth really started flying, I realized it was time to bid my guests goodnight, and I returned to the tent. The party broke up immediately afterward, and my burro guests vanished back into the stillness of the desert night.

The harsh light of the next day made my moonlight encounter with the herd seem like a dream, but the many hoof prints around the picnic table assured me it was not.

As we were breaking camp, the park ranger showed up. I was still wound up about the burros, told the ranger what a wonderful time I'd had with my visitors, and asked if they came from a nearby ranch. He looked at me really strangely when I told him how friendly they were and what a good time we had hanging out. All he said was, "They're wild..." And I realized the burro herd had been an even greater gift than I had thought. They were descendants of the domesticated burros who had helped miners and settlers in the Old West— true survivors of the desert. I felt blessed to have met them.

Rose and quarter horse at Garden of the Gods in Colorado Springs, CO.

THE KINDNESS OF STRANGERS

One of our destinations was the Grand Canyon, and I was really excited to see it, a desire that never truly came to pass as I would spend the next day doing everything I could to get us out of there because the car broke down. It needed a new water pump—a major repair that could not be done at the Grand Canyon service station. We would have to get a tow to the nearest garage that could— about 90 miles away. With our budget, the cost of a tow plus repairs would be more than we could afford. Our trip would have to be cut short, and that made me really sad, and a lot nervous about our budget.

I called my father, but he made it clear we were on our own. So, I decided I needed to call on my courage and the sales skills I used to have when I sold newspaper subscriptions door-to-door as a teenager. I began approaching strangers, telling our story, and asking if anyone would be willing to give us a tow. To my amazement and relief, a couple visiting from nearby Williams, AZ, offered to help us out.

They were so kind. It turned out they did not even have a tow hitch. They wrapped a chain around both bumpers, and we set off on our somewhat scary trip. We had to watch very carefully for any sign of slowing down and not ride the brake, which would put tension on the connection. They took us to the garage they used, where we parked the car since it was after hours. Our good Samaritans would not accept any money from us in thanks.

Williams, Arizona, looked like a small town with one road passing through it. A group of tough-looking bikers were riding up and down the street, and I wondered if we would be okay. The town was small enough that we would definitely be noticed as outsiders. Having been stopped so often on the road by law enforcement, I had gotten pretty paranoid about how we might be perceived. Thankfully, we made it to the motel without incident.

The following day, the garage put the car on the lift to start repairs. A little time passed, and suddenly, I heard yelling. It was my boyfriend telling the mechanics in no uncertain terms to put the car back together—we would take it elsewhere. Apparently, he felt they were trying to cheat us—giving us one price before the car was on the lift and another after it was apart. I thought he had lost his mind. Where were we going to take it, and how?

Still hopping mad, my boyfriend tells me to get in the driver's seat; he will push the car to another garage. As we begin moving at a snail's pace toward our destination two blocks away, I look in the rear-view mirror, and my heart drops into my toes—it's the bikers, and they are getting off their bikes and heading our way. To my surprise, they added their muscle to the pushing, and now we are making better progress. A good lesson mirrored back to never judge a book by its cover!

Suddenly, there were flashing lights in the rear-view mirror. It was the sheriff. I thought for sure this was it. We were going to jail, I'd never make it home, and maybe my father was right.

The sheriff motions everyone out of the way and gently nudges the back bumper. He's going to push us with his vehicle.

With his assistance and our posse of bikers accompanying, I gently steered the car into the next garage, where, thankfully, the repair cost met with my boyfriend's approval. We were back on the road again with one minor challenge: the part they used was not exactly for our car, so the speedometer gave an incorrect reading by 15 mph. Now we had to worry about being stopped for speeding, but at least we could continue, thanks to the kindness of strangers.

CALIFORNIA DREAMING

Our big moment for this cross-country trip would be crossing the state line into California. It was our Shangri-La, perhaps for different reasons.

I had always felt that I had been born just a hair too late to fully participate as a child of the sixties. I was born in 1959 and grew up in Linwood, a beautiful little city of 6000 people, but nonetheless, a backwater of South Jersey where everything new arrived 10 years later.

I was certain I had been meant to be present at Woodstock but took a wrong turn somewhere and got lost on the way to incarnating on the planet. I managed to enjoy and survive a mini-version of Woodstock at my first concert, where years later, I realized that I had narrowly missed dying by a lightning strike, but it was just not the same...

In visiting the fabled California of my dreams, I wanted to see San Francisco, Haight-Asbury, Chinatown, and all the other places I had read about in the cool stories of the sixties and glorified in songs. I wanted to ride on a cable car because, as a kid, I'd left my heart there while listening to Tony Bennett. Thankfully, much as I loved "Mack the Knife," also popular then, it did not evoke a desire to get to know the Jersey Boys.

I did get to do all that and more, but not quite the way I had anticipated. Maybe it had something to do with our ceremonial playing of the Eagle's "Hotel California" when we finally crossed the line into sunny Cali; I had no idea how much my life was about to change.

It started with our seemingly inexplicable decision to stop at a Peddler's Market, which is apparently a West Coast name for what we East Coasters call a flea market.

We had no particular reason for stopping. Acquiring any goods, antique or otherwise, were not included in our plans for car camping. Space was limited.

The place was bustling, but I did not have time to catch more than a glimpse before my boyfriend was ripped from my side by officials who placed him in a communal jail cell with several other unfortunates. It turned out the group was raising money for charity, and bail was set at a dollar. My boyfriend was *not* a happy camper and did not want to make what he considered a forced donation, but I told him that he was an idiot, paid bail, and we moved on.

As we continued on, I spotted a wire cage sitting on the ground. It contained three little kittens up for adoption: two gorgeous little calicos and one blurry grey. The cage was sitting in the sun, and the kittens looked hot. A closer look revealed that they did not have any water, which definitely concerned me.

While I was pondering what to do, my boyfriend was distracted by something else. So he was not by my side when a woman came up with a can of condensed milk, which she poured into a bowl and offered to the kittens, who promptly dove in. I voiced my concerns about them, and the woman said they weren't hers; she had been just passing by like myself. She told me she was involved in animal rescue, and that was why she had gone to get the milk since the kittens looked too young to be completely weaned.

I shared that I missed my cat and a little about our cross-country journey. The rescue lady said maybe I should adopt one. I told her my boyfriend for sure wouldn't let me, but jokingly said maybe I should adopt one for my grandmother and great-aunt as a replacement when I returned since I had heard quite a few stories since my departure about how much they were enjoying "Marky" as they called him.

By this time, my boyfriend was back and had caught wind of the conversation's direction. He was adamant that we were not taking a little kitten along on our journey. I agreed halfheartedly and told the rescue lady that being on the road, we had no carrier to put a little kitten in, and car camping might not be the safest environment for such a wee one.

The rescue lady and I chatted a bit more, and then she said, "I'll be right back, don't leave." Standing by the kittens, I idly wondered which one my Nana and Aunt Tot might like. I decided they would definitely love one of the two beautiful little calicos who had finished their tasty meal of condensed milk, were all washed up, and sleeping soundly like little angels. Not so, the unremarkable gray tabby kitten. He had not been a beauty to start with and was now covered with condensed milk—he looked like he had been wading in it, which was entirely possible. He was very sticky-looking and clearly needed a bath, which he did not seem to think was necessary.

Right about then, the rescue lady returned. She was carrying a handmade wooden and wire mesh cat carrier, which she handed to me as a gift. I had seen them earlier somewhere down the aisle, marked for sale at $10. I was utterly floored. From an outside perspective, someone looking at me would see a hippie-type chick with wild hair and torn jeans traveling the country with her longhaired boyfriend. I did not look like the poster child for responsible pet parenting by a long shot. But she must have seen something in my heart to persuade her to do this. It was a gift of trust, and something fierce inside me rose to the challenge. I turned to my boyfriend and said in a tone of voice he had probably never heard before and did not dare argue with, "Now I have to adopt one."

That decided I went back to the question of which one to choose. I completely discounted the sticky, messy gray male kitten and focused on the two female sleeping calico angels. My deliberations were rudely interrupted by the gray kitten who chose that moment to make his prison break. He must have been plotting it for a while, and now that he had fuel in his belly, he was hitting the road. Somehow, he'd slid himself out between the cage bars and was running across the parking area like he knew exactly where he was going.

The rescue lady recaptured him, and together, we assessed the cage for weakness and repaired the escape area by pushing the two dented bars closer together. Satisfied that we had foiled any future great escapes, we called it good, and I went back to deliberating.

I had almost decided which one when the delinquent gray kitten again made his escape. He headed off in the same direction as before, running as fast as his little legs could carry him. It was as though he had a hot date and was late!

With the little renegade recaptured, reincarcerated, and seemingly restrained once again, I returned to my deliberations. To my amazement, I saw him try again to make a break for it, and I caved. I admired his spunk and self-assurance and decided that the universe was trying to tell me something. To what I am sure was my boyfriend's utter horror, I pointed to the unrepentant little convict who was already wearing prison stripes in the form of tabby markings underneath his coating of condensed milk and said, "That one."

To be continued...

PACHAMAMA'S AMBASSADOR

Storytelling #6

PACHAMAMA'S AMBASSADOR

This past weekend, I taught the final class of the 4-part shamanic series *Spirited Living*.

On Saturday night, we had a potluck dinner before the fire ceremony. As part of the Peruvian shamanic tradition, we have a bowl set aside where each person places something from their plate. This offering of the first and best to Pachamama (Mother Earth) is done in thanksgiving for all we will receive and enjoy with this meal. The Pachamama Bowl is then taken outside, placed on the ground, and left overnight. Usually, the contents are gone by the next day.

We gathered under an almost full moon for our last fire ceremony together. As was usual, my dog, Puma, joined us. However, this time, he snuck away at some point and went off exploring. I had to push my concern away and focus on the ceremony, something I managed to do until he came back quite damp, and I had a moment of angst, wondering what mischief he had been up to, but decided that I would not ask. Sometimes, with dog moms, it is better not to know!

The next day, we had leftovers from the previous night's dinner for lunch, and again, we put out the offering of the Pachamama Bowl. With a sense of satisfaction, I noticed that the previous night's offering was gone.

Later in the day, we again went outside for another fire. This time, we burned individual despachos to give thanks for all we had received in healing during the training and to bring ayni (balance and harmony) to who we were becoming.

I noticed that Puma was eager to join us; he bounded down the stairs ahead of everyone. Once outside, the reason for his haste became clearer; he made a beeline straight for the Pachamama Bowl and quickly gulped down its contents!

The students have now tagged Puma with the nickname "Pachapuma" in honor of his chosen role as representative for Pachamama!

Puma listening for flies.

GOURMET RECYCLING

Like many people, I lead a busy life. As an entrepreneur, I wear many hats in my business and practice, and in my personal life, I am the sole caregiver for several cats and one dog. Sometimes, this means I consume easy-to-fix meals while working at the computer. At the end of the week, it can also mean overlooked leftovers and food items that are not spoiled but not as fresh as I would like.

If the food is not spoiled, rather than tossing it in the garbage or the yard waste recycling bin, I'll first offer it to the local wildlife and see what happens.

This has resulted in some fascinating and unusual discoveries. It is very clear that crows have taste buds and preferences for certain foods. For example, if you put out various disparate items such as fruit, garlic mashed potatoes, cream cheese, and gourmet cheese, most crows will go for the garlic mashed potatoes first, followed by the cheeses, leaving the fruit. Who knew that crows liked dairy products? And it is a very funny sight to see a crow with cream cheese squeezing out either side of his face, trying to grab just a little more before flying off!

Another day's offering included cheez-it type crackers, BBQ potato chips, and cheese puffs. That day afforded me a bird ballet, as the crows would fly off with a tidbit (BBQ chips first, then cheez-its, and finally the puffs), and then a wave of starlings would sweep in, followed by a phalanx of sparrows. As the crows returned, the smaller birds retreated. It looked like a beautiful and carefully choreographed display, and the ground was clear of food in no time.

Today's offering was cherries and cream cheese. Crow alarm calls alerted me to the presence of a different form of wildlife in the courtyard: one of the local cats was sampling the cream cheese! I laughed as I took her picture because I could see the footprints of a former cat resident in the cement next to her.

A while later, one of the three triplet squirrels born in my attic this past spring found himself a treasure trove of cherries. Daintily consuming the first cherry, he neatly buried the pit in one of the cracks in the cement after finishing. Hopefully, we will not have a tree growing there next spring!

GOT 'NIP?

exter lives two doors down from me. Originally, he lived diagonally across the yard, but his people moved, and he was adopted by my cat-friendly neighbors, who are always a soft touch for those left behind. Of course, the benefit to me is that I often end up with extra cat friends who come calling.

Dexter, however, is in a class by himself. His amiable, outgoing personality does not admit a shadow of a doubt that the world will love him. As he is a very large, handsome gray and white cat with a sort of bumbling and insistent charm, most of the world seems to agree with him, myself included.

My first introduction to Dexter was as I dug a hole to plant a newly acquired addition to the garden. Suddenly, this strange cat was right next to me, peering into the hole with intense concentration as though he was an inspector for Better Homes and Gardens. So intense was his interest that I had to elbow him back from the hole as I dug because I was concerned that I was going to accidentally stab him with the Japanese digging knife I was using!

From then on, Dexter regularly visited to see what I was up to and quickly discovered that I had a secret stash of catnip in my garage. I have a student who is a gardening wonder and brings me fresh stems of catnip in season. I take these fragrant offerings, hang them to dry, and then store them in the garage where my cats can't get to them. This way, I can dole the catnip out in measured doses rather than having an entire household turn into feline junkies on a bender for days.

I left the garage door open one day, and Dexter wandered in and discovered the stash. He ripped the bag down and proceeded to have a glorious time. The next time I saw him the garage door was closed, but Dexter was having none of it. Meowing loudly and longingly, he proceeded to tell me just how miserable his lot in life was without that luscious scent that rolled up warm radiators, sunshine, cushiony beds, and sardines on toast into one whisker-twitching burst of glorious nirvana. Listening to him made me yearn momentarily for my long-gone, stupefied early college years! So, I caved and gave him a hit of my super cat stash, which was my undoing. Now, every time Dexter sees me outside, he wants what he knows I've got. I am now his favorite dealer of choice.

Dexter knew I was taking these photos. Rather than being ashamed of his addiction, he decided that any fame is better than no fame at all. So, here he is looking rather like a furry version of Carmen Miranda with a catnip stem, rather than a rose, clamped in his teeth!

RACCOON AND THE GREAT SQUIRREL BANK ROBBERY

I t's not every day that you witness a bank robbery in broad daylight or that the perp gets away with the goods despite photographic evidence of the crime.

Unusually, instead of the crime ending with a chase scene, it began with one—from my kitchen window, I saw a squirrel racing across the courtyard with a raccoon in hot pursuit. As the squirrel vanished around the corner, the raccoon came to a stop. Quickly, quietly, and efficiently, every single one of the squirrel's food banks, contents painstakingly gathered and stored underground for a rainy day, was plundered and consumed.

Having disposed of the evidence, the masked thief strolled casually across the courtyard, unconcerned that I had opened a window and was clicking away with my camera. And why should he be? No evidence of a crime remained, and I doubted the squirrel would take the issue up with him.

As the raccoon sauntered toward the back fence, I opened another window with a better view. Hanging out the window, clicking away, I sensed a presence by my elbow. It was my dog,

Puma. He made no sound, but I could feel the intensity of his focus.

Puma looking cool.

I have to give him credit; Puma has gamely adjusted to every eccentricity in my household since I first adopted him from a shelter in Montana. When he arrived in Seattle, he was a Western rural dog who had never experienced big city living, and to him, raccoons were varmints.

The Cat Tribe clockwise from left: Sand, Saqqara, Kiya (napping with abandon), half bobcat Cougar, and Shaman with his favorite toy.

My first inkling that Puma and I were not on the same page concerning wildlife preservation came late one night. My cats began crazily freaking out and bouncing off the walls while simultaneously, Puma began to growl, something he never does. And it was a growl that really meant business.

With my hair almost standing on end, I was convinced that we were seriously under attack by an unknown threat. I could hear sounds coming from the back stairs, which meant I must have left the back door open. Oh dear. Bravely grasping my tiny flashlight and wishing it was much more substantial as a potential weapon, I headed to the back door, Puma at my side.

Placing my hand on the doorknob, I could feel all the cats take a deep breath (and I'm sure I did, too), and then I did the one thing that convinced Puma I had lost my mind: I put him behind me and made him sit. I clearly heard him say, "Are you nuts?!" But, bless him, he did it.

As I gingerly opened the door, the small beam of my flashlight illuminated the masked face of our intruder, a very large raccoon who was busily tearing into and consuming the samples of high-quality cat and dog food I had so conveniently left on the stairs for her.

With Puma guarding my back, I drew myself up to full height from the hunting crouch I had not realized I had assumed and sternly told the bandit, "I'm going to count to three, and I expect you to put down the goods, and exit the building." There was a part of me that wondered what I thought I was going to do on three, but I squelched it. The best offense is a good bluff.

The raccoon thought it over and decided that perhaps I meant business. But she let me know that she did not consider me a serious threat by slowly sauntering down the stairs and out of the building. The cats stood down from red alert and, still shaking his head over his human's apparent daftness, Puma went back to bed. In his mind, I should have let him at the varmint.

Not long after, Puma had his chance. We were in the backyard when suddenly he dashed out of sight around the side of the building. Rounding the corner, I discovered Puma had treed two unhappy teenage raccoon twins. Puma was grievously disappointed when I pulled him away—he was having fun.

But the worst was yet to come.

One day, out for our daily walk, I noticed a raccoon entering a neighbor's house through the cat door. Easily picturing the dismay of their multi-cat household, I returned home to leave a message regarding their intruder and grabbed my camera. As

Puma and I left the house again, I was surprised to see the raccoon drinking water from the small pond behind the iron gates of my next-door neighbor's front yard.

The raccoon looked awful; he had open wounds, and many areas of fur were missing. Apparently, he had been hit by a car and dragged. He moved stiffly and was in pain, and I felt sorry for him.

But not Puma. He wanted a piece of that injured raccoon but was hesitant because he knew I did not share his perspective. The raccoon was calm, secure in knowing that a fence separated him from disapproving Puma. Sensing my compassion, the raccoon sent me a pleading look, and I caved.

Putting Puma on sit once again (and I had to tell him twice because he genuinely did not want to), I reached into the bag I carried and pulled out my newly purchased deli sandwich—the one I had been looking forward to having for lunch.

Puma shot me a look of pure disbelief as I sacrificed half of my sandwich, tossing it through the gate to the eager raccoon. I just looked at Puma and shrugged.

All those shared encounters flashed through my mind as Puma and I hung out the window, observing the current raccoon nonchalantly stroll across my garage roof, the same masked bandit who had pillaged that poor squirrel's rainy-day food bank.

As we watched the raccoon disappear over the roof peak, presumably to knock over another hardworking squirrel's stash, I put my arm around Puma and gave him a quick hug of acknowledgment. For the first time, we were in agreement—this raccoon was a thieving varmint.

Raccoon Varmint making his escape across the garage roof.

CALIFORNIA DREAMING CONTINUED

At the end of last month's *Storytelling*, I left you with a cliffhanger at the conclusion of "California Dreamin." I had just made the fateful decision to adopt the little gray kitten, coated in condensed milk, who had already made several prison breaks from his cage.

With cat carrier in hand and little gray kitten safely incarcerated inside for the moment, I paused to assess what I had gotten myself into and what steps to take next. Looking more closely at the kitten, I realized he was younger than I had thought. I was not sure he was up for solid food quite yet. And we were car camping in campgrounds—I was going to need some way to keep an eye on him—he could not live in the carrier all the time.

So, the first step was to find a pet store. Mind you, we knew nothing of the area, yet somehow, we managed to locate one where I purchased a harness intended for a Chihuahua from a very amused salesperson. It was the smallest they had, but it was still quite large for the small kitten, so I had to cut it down a bit to get it to fit a bit more snuggly. I offered up a prayer that the kitten's escape artist tendencies did not include a Houdini-like ability to wriggle out of his harness restraint.

I also purchased a leash, long cord, canned cat food, and some kitten milk replacer. They did not have a litter box small enough to fit inside the wooden carrier, which was palatial compared to the size of the kitten. Thankful for the ingenuity of my mother, who I had learned a few things from while growing up with our menagerie, a trip to the supermarket yielded a storage container that would do quite well for the litter pan, and I also picked up some all-meat baby food. I now felt better prepared for caring for my newly acquired baby feline, whom I was sure my grandmother and aunt would love. In the meantime, he needed a name, so I called him Peddler after the West Coast flea market he'd come from.

When we set up the tent that night, it had a new piece of furniture: the cat carrier, which was now Peddler's new bedroom quarters. When the food dish, water bowl, litter box, and sleeping quarters were all set up, there was still room left over since he was so small. I felt a bit of unease. Was I really going to be able to give him the care he needed?

As we made dinner preparations, I put little Peddler in his harness, clipped on his leash, and tied one end of the tether to the leash and the other to the picnic table. I kept a close eye on him until I was sure he did not intend to shuck it and run into the woods.

A little bit later, I became aware that I did not see him running around. My heart stopped but resumed beating once I followed the tether to its end. Peddler had not escaped. However, he had decided it was a good time to explore the intricacies of the internal combustion engine. He had climbed inside the engine compartment of the '63 Chevy, which was not a good place to be. Thankfully an engine of that vintage is a lot less complex than the cars of today. I extracted him without much difficulty but with one major difference. He no longer had a coating of condensed milk since I had cleaned him off earlier; now, his fur was coated with black oil. I was not a happy camper and scolded him thoroughly as we marched off to the camp's shower facilities. When Peddler and I finally emerged from the shower building a bit later, dripping wet and tired, a somewhat startled man who saw us remarked, "I've heard of togetherness, but *this* is ridiculous." I am sure that Peddler wholeheartedly agreed with him.

It took one more dive into the engine and one more immediate shower before Peddler decided that car engines were best left alone.

One of the major hurdles I encountered on our trip was what to do with Peddler during our planned visit to Disneyland—something my boyfriend and I had really been looking forward to. There was no way I would consider leaving Peddler in the car. I wondered whether I should try to smuggle little Peddler into Disneyland and risk us all getting thrown out of the park. If I did smuggle him in, I would not be going on the rides with my boyfriend since there was no way I'd want to subject Peddler to being spun and whipped around in circles.

As a child, I lived for Sunday nights when the *Wonderful World of Disney* was on. I loved it all—the dramas and the animal documentaries—and had always wondered what it would be like to actually go in person. It would be magical to see the animatronic parrots, the ghostly dancers, and the jungle ride with the elephant family, but if I couldn't take Peddler with me, then I wasn't going, and my boyfriend was going to be very upset since he hadn't wanted him to join us in the first place.

When we arrived at Disneyland, I wrapped Peddler in his swaddling blanket and tucked him into my capacious purse.

As we neared the entrance, to my surprise, I saw that Disneyland had a place where you could board your animal companion for the day, and it was only a dollar!

The folks working there assured me that Peddler would have the complete spa treatment. They took in all his supplies, noted how often he needed to be fed, and reassured me that a veterinarian was on staff if needed. It may have been a marketing ploy, but the child in me that had worshipped at the altar of all things animal and Disney said a prayer of gratitude. Thank you, Walt Disney!

Retrieving little Peddler after our Disneyland adventure, I realized while making camp for the night that he needed a different name since he was not answering to the one I had so quickly bestowed upon him. When I called his name it went completely over his head—literally. I wondered whether he did not like the name or if it simply did not resonate with who he was. After all, I had named him after the place where I found him rather than waiting to get to know who he was as an individual.

So I turned my mind to what was most notable about him, and one thing stood out—his eyes were starting to change color to the green they would eventually be. The ragged way the color in the irises was distributed looked like the shape of stars. Which reminded me that I had brought a small book on constellations on the trip with me—perhaps I could find a name for him there.

In rifling through the book, one constellation stood out from all the rest—the pulsating binary star constellation Lepus.

Lepus is Latin for rabbit (or hare) and seemed to suit him since he bounced around in a kind of hopping motion when he felt particularly exuberant. It felt like a fit, but I decided that he should be the judge this time. He was off exploring, again on his lead and halter, so I called out to him, "Lepus!" He immediately turned and ran back to me. From that moment on he always answered to Lepus, I never had to teach him. Name approved.

Our next stop was the fabled city of cable cars, Chinatown, Haight-Asbury, and Fisherman's Wharf—San Francisco, here we come—and little Lepus went with us.

I bundled him up in a towel, which served as his blanket, and the moment we arrived at Fisherman's Wharf, I bought us a shrimp cocktail and offered him a ginormous shrimp with a flourish. His little furry face lit up; he looked like the gates of heaven had opened and ushered him in before he dove into the shrimp with eager abandon. For the rest of his life, Lepus was a fan of trying new things, especially when it came to food.

Our time in San Francisco was fun, made even more so because of Lepus. Despite our looking like hippies, having the little guy along caused other animal lovers to gravitate toward us.

Pretty soon, we had a well-established routine going: setting up camp each night, breaking it down in the morning, and Lepus blended in seamlessly. He never cried when I put him in the carrier, nor when we spent hours in the car traveling, a habit that thankfully remained with him for life.

All good things come to an end, and our trip ended sooner than expected. My boyfriend discovered that he had landed his dream summer job, and we had to get back immediately. Immediately meant three days of fairly nonstop driving, shared between us, and through it all, Lepus was a trooper.

While on the road, I realized that our idyllic time together was ending. When I returned I would need to retrieve Marquis and gift Lepus to my grandmother and my aunt, and I felt really sad. Unlike Marquis, Lepus had really bonded to me and me alone.

An earlier call to my grandmother and aunt had revealed that they were having a wonderful time hosting Marquis and were full of stories about him. Maybe they might want to keep him?

When I arrived at their house I saw Marquis had taken over the place and settled in quite comfortably. I had wondered if he might have been bored after all the excitement of dorm living during his formative months, but apparently, he was an adaptive fellow. Sprawled across the top of their best chair, now covered with a towel so that his claws would not damage it, Marquis radiated goodwill and self-satisfaction with all the goodies he was being offered. He clearly had the run of the place and my grandmother's and aunt's hearts.

They reported two endearing quirks. Marquis liked to come up behind a guest seated on the sofa, plant a paw on them, and wash their hair. The other habit they laughingly reported was that guests had to watch their cigarette packs because Marquis would try to steal a cigarette. Apparently, he had acquired another bad habit in the dorm that I was unaware of.

They were two quirks he kept his entire life—ones that always made my grandmother and aunt laugh. Yes, you guessed it, Marquis stayed with them. It was an arrangement that seemed to suit everyone. They doted on him, and like a supremely benevolent, affectionate, and kindly feline king, he adored the attention.

Years later, when my aunt passed away, my grandmother took it hard. They were raised together as children and returned to live together when both were widowed at a fairly young age.

My grandmother moved from South Jersey to Philadelphia at my mother's urging, and Marquis went with her. When I visited, it was clear that he loved my grandmother, and she loved him. It eased my heart to see that Marquis seemed content with my life choice for him so long ago.

Eventually, my grandmother developed Alzheimer's and moved in with my mother. By that time, my mother was deeply into breeding show cats, and while she would have welcomed him, it was clear that I needed to take Marquis back. I had added a few more cats by then, but nothing like the numbers at my mother's house, where he would receive little individual attention. It seemed the least I could do for him in his senior years.

And so, for a little longer, Marquis returned to Massachusetts, the state of his birth, and took up a position on my sofa where he washed guests' hair and stole their cigarettes (and mine).

I had also added some pet mice to my menagerie, and he loved watching them. One day, one escaped; I have no idea how. My first awareness that the mouse was not in the tank was when Marquis threw up an entire dead mouse. Apparently, he had hidden depths as a hunter, if not a digester, of mice.

One day, I noticed a growth on his face, and it turned out to be cancerous. I was devastated. Marquis was a link to my early college life, my departed aunt, and a grandmother who was no longer available due to her illness.

At that time, veterinary medicine could do little for him, so I began looking into alternatives. Very little was available then for people and less for animals. I added all kinds of chopped dried herbs to his food, which he valiantly ate, and even had a sound healer come by. Nothing helped—the tumor grew larger. Half his food was herbs by now, and it finally was too much for him. He could no longer eat without pain, and I knew that it was goodbye—we had spun his life out as far as we could, and he was ready to leave.

Marquis, I am grateful to you for teaching me how to embrace what life offers with grace, joy, and a wicked sense of humor. I hope you are enjoying a heck of a party wherever the journey takes you next!

THE RETURN

After our big adventure cross-country, Lepus and I spent the summer at my mother's house in South Jersey.

My sister Francine and little Lepus.

My boyfriend's summer job as a lifeguard was back in Massachusetts. The plan was that when school resumed, the four of us would share an apartment: my boyfriend, my freshman-year best girlfriend, and her boyfriend, who also happened to be my boyfriend's best friend and roommate—and Lepus, of course.

I was very much in love. My boyfriend and I wrote letters back and forth throughout the summer. I would always save his letter until the end of the day when I could relax and give it my full attention.

Two weeks before school started, I received another letter from him and savored the anticipation. When I finally opened it, I was devastated to discover that he had written to tell me that he had found someone else and that they would be moving in with our friends.

My heart was in pieces, and I had a real problem: where would I live, and how would I find a place from 250 miles away? Nice off-campus places were usually spoken for long before now, and dorm life was out of the question with Lepus.

I tried calling my boyfriend, and his mother stonewalled me. When I finally found a way around her by having my younger sister call, I guilted him into finding me a place to live—which he did. When he told me where it was located, my heart sank. It was a ground-floor apartment in a beautiful, stately three-story building with bay windows, but it was also situated near Kilby Street—an area of town that Clarkies (students) had been told to avoid at all costs since it was a supposed hotbed of drugs and crime. But I had no other choice.

Broken-hearted, I cried every day, and Lepus was my rock in the painful uncertainty of our future. He would climb into my lap and allow me to hug him while I soaked his fur with my tears. Every night, he laid himself in my arms like a teddy bear.

Leaving day arrived, and my father and I loaded up the van with some basic furniture and Lepus and I returned to Massachusetts for what was going to have been the start of a glorious new year.

Instead, as Lepus and I looked around our new, sparsely furnished, and possibly dangerous new home, I realized I was essentially friendless. I had spent so much time as part of a couple my freshman year, that I had not cultivated friendships outside of the one with my now ex-best friend and ex-boyfriend. Lepus and I were on our own.

to be continued...

LIFE ON THE EDGE

Storytelling #7

LIFE ON THE EDGE

A quick recap of where we left off in our last story, the continuation of "California Dreaming":

I made the fateful decision to adopt the little grey kitten I eventually named Lepus while on a car camping road trip through California with my boyfriend. After several adventures adjusting to life on the road, Lepus and I returned to my family home in South Jersey for the summer, while my boyfriend returned to Mass. and his summer job. In the fall, the plan was that Lepus and I would move in with my boyfriend, my best girlfriend and my boyfriend's best friend. Two weeks before I was to return to college, all that changed. Instead, at the conclusion of the last story, Lepus and I found ourselves living alone in a less-than-safe neighborhood.

LIFE ON THE EDGE

The apartment that Lepus and I now lived in was on the ground floor. My landlords were very nice and brought me up to speed on the other tenants. They told me that the apartment across the hallway was rented but currently unoccupied. Apparently, it belonged to a young woman who had had some kind of terrible accident that she was recovering from.

My new landlords expressed some concern about my living alone. They said the neighborhood was no longer a truly safe place to live. They cautioned me not to leave the windows open or go out at night. Since I did not have a car and would have to transport my laundry on my bike, living there was sounding more and more unnerving. I took to sleeping with a knife near my bed, just in case.

The only other neighbors I met were the couple who lived upstairs. She was a schoolteacher, and while I don't recall what her husband did for a living, I definitely remember his asking if I minded bagpipe music since he enjoyed listening to it first thing on a Saturday morning. I reassured him that I actually enjoyed it, and every Saturday morning, right on time, the skirling sound of bagpipes would fill the hallway for an hour.

Other than occasional conversations with my bagpipe-music-playing neighbor, Lepus and I lived lonely lives. During the day, I went to classes and worked in the campus kitchen, and when I returned home, Lepus would be standing at the door waiting to greet me. It was pretty quiet for him, too.

There were definitely some weird moments living there. Like the night I heard a knock on my door at 10:00 p.m. My upstairs, married male neighbor told me he had just gotten back from the pub. He asked if he could come in, and since he had been in my place in the past, I thought nothing of it.

We were having a normal conversation while standing in the middle of my living room when he suddenly picked me up and held me over his head while telling me how much he liked me. Between the declaration and his breath, I realized that he was drunk.

From my superior height advantage, I forcefully told him to put me down. Once I had my feet back on the floor, I gave him a lecture on how stupid it would be to have an affair with someone whose wife was right upstairs and that I was not interested in married men. I told him he would be glad in the morning that I sent him home and that we would not revisit this again. He did apologize the next day and insisted on inviting me to breakfast with him and his wife. That was not uncomfortable at all…

Then there was the time there was a power failure after dark, and there was no one else in the building but Lepus and me. I called a friend just to have someone on the line so I did not feel quite so nervous.

The hardest to bear during all this was going to the free movies at the college theater. Not only did I have to go alone, but I also had to endure knowing that the projectionist was my ex-boyfriend and his new girlfriend was sharing the projection booth with him instead of me. The absolute worst was the night the college screened the romantic tragedy *Casablanca*. I came home in tears, but Lepus was there, faithfully waiting for me, and once again, he curled up in my lap and allowed my tears to drench his fur.

Around this time, I also came down with a really bad flu. I was so sick that I could not leave my bed other than to take care of necessities like feeding Lepus—my loving companion through thick and thin. He nursed me through three really awful days, comforting me when I felt vulnerable and very sorry for myself. I was so sick I can recall asking myself if something dire happened to me, how would anyone know, and who would take care of Lepus?

Thankfully, I recovered, and day by day—with Lepus' support —I gradually picked up the pieces of my life and started to move forward.

And I thought it might all work out until one day, I came home, and Lepus was at the door to greet me as usual, but this time, he was loudly meowing up a storm—something he had never done before. His face had a stricken expression, his eyes were huge, and his whiskers stood straight out. With every meow, I knew he was urgently trying to tell me something. Somehow, I received the information that a stranger had been in *our* home, which was very scary for him. A careful look around my few possessions verified that three things were missing. I had forgotten about the open window, and someone had taken advantage of it. They were watching the house—and us.

I immediately called my landlords, who came right over, bless them. Nothing had been damaged when the intruders gained access, but I no longer felt safe and was really worried about Lepus. He assured me he had hidden, but I would never have forgiven myself if something had happened to him.

I asked my landlords if they minded if I got a dog, and they gave their blessing.

Rose and Wulfgar

So, I adopted a lovely young black springer spaniel-type dog from the city shelter. I named him Wulfgar, Wolfie for short. He was only about 10 months old, full of joy, and still a puppy at heart. Lepus and he got along fine, but Wolfie did not handle being left alone for hours at a time well and tore a hole in my chair. The windowsills were not looking too good either. I now know that he had separation anxiety, but at the time, I was clueless.

As I look back on my younger self from the much wiser and far more educated perspective that almost 40 years can offer, there are many things I would have done differently from this time in my life. I was unaware of crate training or how to find someone who could help even if I had the money, so I came up with my own not-so-good solution.

Given how many dogs there were in Worcester roaming the streets and on campus, I figured that Wolfie must have been one of those, so I started bringing him to campus and letting him run with the other campus dogs while I was in class. He had no trouble finding his way home; one day, he brought a dog friend with him. But this was not working the way I had hoped. Having him roaming the streets during the day was not good for either of us—I constantly worried about him. It was clear that he was not going to be a guard dog, and sadly I realized that I had to send him back to the shelter and hope that someone else would give him a better home.

Shortly after returning Wolfie, life started to get really strange. I would find things in the hallway that told me that someone was coming in that did not live there and my place seemed to be the one they were interested in. By this point, I was not sleeping well. As we approached the season of winter daylight hours were getting shorter and shorter, and I would soon be coming home after dark. Once snow fell, I could not ride my bike to and from school; I would have to walk. My anxiety level continued to go up.

I decided that I needed to seriously begin looking for another place for us to live, hopefully closer to campus and in a safer neighborhood. However, mid-semester was not the best time to start looking. I needed roommates to afford rent, and many places did not accept pets, but living anywhere without Lepus was not an option.

And then a lot of things happened quickly.

One morning, I opened my apartment door and discovered two kittens sleeping on my doormat in the hallway. They immediately woke up and marched in like they owned the place. One was a calico female, the other a tabby. I told them they could not stay and promptly put them out on the porch. To this day, I have no idea how they managed to arrive at my door. The upstairs neighbors disavowed any knowledge of them, and the front door to the house appeared to be locked.

In retrospect, I don't know what I was thinking to put them outside, even if it was where I felt they had come from. I can only assume the loss of sleep and anxiety had finally taken its toll. What I did know is that not knowing how they got there on top of the other strange things that had been happening was really starting to creep me out. It was enough of a challenge taking care of myself and Lepus, and I simply did not feel I could handle much more.

The following day, I heard the pitiful sound of a kitten crying coming from underneath the house. After hours of searching, I finally found someone with a key and rescued the little calico kitten from the cellar. I had no idea how she had gotten herself locked in—another mystery I would never solve. Sadly, I never saw the little tabby again.

By this point, I had come to my senses and realized I could not put the calico kitten back out on the street—she clearly did not have a home.

Madame Calico did not seem to care that she was now solo, she made herself at home, and Lepus suddenly found himself on the outside looking in. When I sat down, Madame Calico would take over my lap. When it was bedtime, she curled under my chin and purred happily. Poor Lepus would stand there with such a sad expression; it broke my heart. When I moved Madame Calico, she'd simply march resolutely back and take over again. She had a will of iron, and in the future, whenever I think of calico cat determination, I will always remember her. She made it clear that she was in charge even though she could not have been more than 12 weeks old. The worst was the look she would give Lepus. It was clear that she knew that she was putting him to the side, and she reveled in her power. I resolved to find her another home as soon as possible.

And then suddenly, everything kicked into overdrive. At last, I found a potential new place to live a few blocks from campus. Nice apartment in a triple-decker on the second floor (by this time, I was definitely disenchanted with first-floor living). The rent was affordable, and when I was interviewed by my potential new roommates, they said they liked cats. However, I was warned that the lease said no pets, but they figured that what the landlord did not know would not hurt him; they were prepared to hide Lepus if necessary, which was heartwarming.

However, there were two more hurdles before it was a done deal. Because I was moving from a single apartment to a shared one, I had a bit more furniture than the average college student. The room that my prospective new roommates showed me was not large enough to fit it all. I remarked that the front sitting room had the amount of space that I needed, but their male roommate currently occupied it. I don't quite recall how it all went down, but the end result was they decided to ask him to move out and invited me to take his place.

The second hurdle was an emotional one. The back of Lepus' and my new residence-to-be was directly across the street from where my ex-boyfriend and new girlfriend lived. The same shared residence of what had become my ex-best friend and her boyfriend, who had told me that while they did not like my ex's girlfriend, they did not want to create waves by hanging out with me since the new girlfriend was jealous of me. There was no way to avoid occasionally seeing members of this unholy quartet, but I decided that I was willing to brave it, and perhaps I could eke out some feeling of revenge. Having the jilted ex-girlfriend parked across the street must be somewhat disturbing. Indeed, later, the Girlfriend accused me of having deliberately planned it that way. I have to say that, spitefully, I did derive some small satisfaction from being a spoke in the wheel.

Without a car I had no way to get myself moved, and much to my grateful surprise, my boss and one of my co-workers volunteered themselves and the college van. This happened so fast that I did not have time to find Madame Calico a proper new home. My new roommates were adamant that I could not move in with two cats—that would be over the top lease-wise as the landlords were not pet-friendly at all—they were not willing to accept two cats.

I was between a rock and a hard spot. There was no way that Lepus and I could continue to live where we were. And there were no other options than the apartment I had already agreed to move into. To say I was stressed was putting it mildly.

Moving day arrived, and I still could not find Madame Calico a home. I was frantic. Everything was in the van, and we were getting ready to leave. Madame Calico was the last to leave the house with me. I had her in my arms and was standing on the sidewalk, still not knowing what to do, when a girl about 10 stopped and remarked how beautiful she was. I impulsively asked her if she wanted a kitten, and she looked delighted and said, "Yes!" So I handed her Madame Calico, and she lovingly cradled her over her shoulder.

As the young girl walked away with her new friend, I prayed that what I had just done was supported by kind Providence rather than being an act of carelessness on my part. Over the years, I have done much personal clearing work around that moment, but I will never forget the stunned look of betrayal on Madame Calico's face. I hope she eventually forgave me. Maybe someday I will forgive myself.

DINNER PARTY ON BEAVER STREET

Lepus and I moved into our new residence on Beaver Street without fanfare, especially since he was trying to keep a low profile.

The sitting room that became my bedroom was lovely and sunny, with a large bay window, but it lacked a door because it had never been intended to be a sleeping space. Instead, I used the two wooden pillars on either side of the entrance to anchor a wire cable, on which I strung safety pins and hung my father's old green army blanket as a curtain. That old blanket was my only privacy barrier for my entire college career.

Triple-deckers were initially built as housing for the immigrant mill workers who made Worcester great in the day. Despite being essentially housing for the lower class, they were built to last and had a lot of charm. Most of the woodwork was original, but in this unit, someone (probably a college student) had been inspired to paint the pass-through between the kitchen and the dining room a memorable shade of bubble gum pink.

The kitchen stove was also our space heater, and Lepus quickly became a fixture next to the tea kettle.

My new roommates liked to cook, so in the spirit of cama-raderie, I took turns cooking and shopping. I even volunteered to cook for a dinner party where we could invite our friends. By the time we finished with the guest list, 18 people were coming. Perversely, I had decided to invite my ex-boyfriend and the Girlfriend. Completely unexpectedly, they accepted, which I heard was more my ex's idea than the Girlfriend's.

When dinner party night arrived, we filled the kitchen with tables and chairs. It was so crowded that I had to serve directly from the stove, and the steam fogged all the windows. In addition to the main course of stuffed eggplant, I had also prepared stuffed mushrooms as the appetizer—a specialty I had learned to make as a teenager while working as a caterer's assistant.

After all these years, much of the dinner is a blur, but one thing stands out in my memory. Halfway through dinner, my ex and his girlfriend abruptly left. Later, I heard that my ex left because he became ill with a severe digestive upset, which lasted for a day or two. My spy informed me that the Girl-friend was certain that I had tried to poison my ex, a thought that I can assure you all had not even entered my mind. But in all honesty, the suffering he endured was somewhat consoling...

NO ONE LEFT BEHIND

The holidays were approaching, and that meant I needed to make travel plans to be with my family. My roommates would also be gone, so I needed to figure something out for Lepus. Since I did not have a car, I could not take him with me, and boarding him at the vet was something I knew he did not want. My ex and the Girlfriend were staying in town, and since I felt like he at least owed me this, I asked my ex if he would be willing to take Lepus in while I was gone and care for him. He agreed.

It was the first time Lepus and I would be parted since he had come into my life, but I dropped him off at my ex's in a relatively peaceful frame of mind since he and Lepus were hardly strangers.

Well, as it turned out, I had forgotten to factor in something important, and I would not discover what that was until after I picked Lepus up. I was so happy to see him again—it was a very happy reunion for us both, and I thought all was fine.

A few days later, I heard the actual story. Not long after I safely dropped him off, Lepus took matters into his own paws and escaped from the house. And despite everyone's efforts to find him over the next few days, he remained unaccounted for until shortly before I returned to pick him up. An hour before my arrival, Lepus appeared at the door to be placed in his cat carrier. My spy told me that my ex had been frantic, dreading how to break the news that the cat I loved so much was gone.

Listening to the tale of Lepus' defection, I laughed at myself. What had I been thinking when I set this up with my ex? Over the past few months, Lepus had steadfastly held space for me every time I cried over the loss of my boyfriend. Over that time, Lepus had probably wrung a small, salty sea of my grieving tears out of his fur. He had chosen a side and decided to support me, and he was obviously much better at boundaries than I.

When I checked in with Lepus about all of this, he made it clear to me that there was no way he was going to stay with the guy who had thrown me over for someone else. Our connection was so strong that he knew exactly when I was returning. Lepus told me we were a team, and he had my back. From then on, I never left him behind; we always traveled together.

SHAMANIC JOURNEYS AND CEREMONIES WITH ANIMALS

Wen I first began studying shamanism and learned how to journey outside of time and space, it never occurred to me that it might be possible for animals to journey as well or that they might want to participate.

My first experience was with client cat Cozee. During her session, I embarked on a shamanic journey to bring back information and healing for her. To my surprise, I discovered Cozee following along with me as I traveled down the stone tunnels deep into the earth. When we got to the river where I usually immersed myself to travel to see the Keeper of the Lower World cat Cozee understandably did not want to get in the water. So, instead, we traveled there and back by small boat so that she could stay dry.

I shared all that had happened with Cozee's person, including her inserting herself in the journey, and thought no more of it.

A few days later, Cozee's person contacted me to say that since her session, Cozee had taken to sitting in the bathtub and not coming out for hours, something she had never done before.

My client asked if I had any idea why. I had to laugh—Cozee had enjoyed the journey so much that she was now trying to journey by herself!

Another fascinating experience occurred during a three-day workshop called *Horses as Healers and Teachers*. The horse teachers were very used to working with corporate humans around leadership issues but had not previously been exposed to shamanic practices, so I was very interested to see how they would respond.

The workshop included a shamanic journey so attendees could discover their power animals and begin working with them. It was a lovely summer's day, so we sat outside on the grass under the shade of a tree, quite close to the paddock where two of the horses were peacefully grazing. It was a wonderful setting, and I was looking forward to bringing everyone on the journey.

At the time, I was still relying on the sound of my rattle to guide folks there and back. I had never used it near horses before, so as I began rattling, I was paying close attention to see if they would be uneasy since it could sound like a rattlesnake—which all horses seem to instinctively fear.

The horses were intrigued but calm, so I added the spoken part of the journey, guiding folks to the place in the journey where they call to their power animal to join them. Meeting your power animal for the first time can be a very powerful experience; truly connecting with the animal means experiencing life through their eyes and actions. I raised my voice and powerfully exhorted the students and their power animals to "Run, fly, swim!"

I felt it before I heard it—a trembling of the earth where I sat. As I looked up, I saw all the students with eyes closed, and the two horses were wildly galloping around the paddock, kicking up their heels, and having a great time. It was their hooves that were making the earth tremble. I was so surprised I had to sharply redirect my attention back to keeping the beat with my rattle. The sound of their hooves combined with it was exquisitely beautiful, and I felt so grateful for the moment. But the horses were not yet done.

When I felt the time was right to switch gears in the journey, I cued the students with, "And now you are thirsty. Find water and drink." To my complete and utter amazement, both horses stopped running right in front of me and dipped their heads down to the grass. Both heads popped up sharply and swiveled to look right at me. They clearly said, "But there's no water here." Only then did I realize that the horses were actively participating in the journey. I almost dropped my rattle. Who knew?

Throughout the weekend, the horses were very interested and participatory, but they took it to another level when it came time for us to join in ceremony and bring our collected prayers to fire.

I opened sacred space, the place between the worlds where spirit and physical world can intermingle, by calling to the Four Directions. The horses had the option to be with us if they wished, or they could go out of the arena into the pasture. When planning this, I was concerned that they might be frightened by the fire, but apparently, that does not apply to sacred fire.

Lead mare Reba had my back.

As the people gathered in a circle around the fire, lead mare Reba, who had had my back the entire time, took up a position in one corner of the arena, and three other horses followed suit, each in a different direction. They were holding space for the ceremony! I felt such a sense of awe. What most people might consider a fairy tale was happening right before my eyes.

And just when I thought it could not get any more heart-poundingly spiritual, Savannah—a black mare who had previously demonstrated a strong interest in all things energy—joined us. While I continued to rattle, she stood next to me, her front hooves even with the human feet on either side. And she stayed with us the entire time, gazing into the fire, impervious to the smoke, hooves so close at times that I worried a spark might lick her ankles.

When the ceremony was complete, there was such a sense of peace and connection that no one wanted to leave. The people and the horses had truly come together as one.

AWAKENING OWL MEDICINE

I was having one of those days, feeling a little down and very rushed and overwhelmed. As Puma and I were midway through our usual stroll around the neighborhood, I became aware of a small group of teenage boys. They were clustered together by the path that meanders through Whale Tail Park, armed with cameras and cell phones, taking pictures upward into the branches of a cedar tree. I might have thought nothing of it if I had not overhead the word "owl."

Responding to my enthusiasm, the teenagers were kind enough to carefully guide my eyes to where a gorgeous barred owl was trying to take a daytime nap.

Deliberately choosing to upend my schedule, Puma and I hurried back to retrieve my camera. While I have occasionally heard Western screech owls in my neighborhood, I have never seen a wild owl on our walks. Here was my first opportunity to photograph one!

Upon returning, I put Puma on down-stay and angled for the best shot possible. It was not easy. Besides the limitations of my neck injury, numerous branches were in the way, and the lighting was quite dim. I only managed to get a few shots before Owl swiveled his head around; it was now facing backward.

For a while, shots of the back of his head were all I could obtain, so I waited patiently until he finally resumed a face-forward position. Eyes tightly closed, he attempted to ignore the crowd of amateur paparazzi who passed beneath his tree bedroom. I was encouraged by how many people excitedly ran off to tell others. Seeing the wonder and awe he was greeted with and the care everyone took to speak as quietly as possible to not disturb him was truly inspiring. Having acute hearing, I am sure he could hear us all quite well if he wished, but I hoped he could angle the feathers around his ear holes so that he had the owl equivalent of cotton balls muffling our noise.

Just when I was wishing that I could get a shot that did not include so many branches, all of which seemed to block some part of his handsome face, one man called me over to stand about 20 feet back up a slight incline where I discovered I could see the owl in all his magnificence. Score one for the kindness of strangers and the maxim that sometimes you are too close to see the forest for the trees. In my desire to get as close as possible I had neglected a cardinal rule of photography, to explore other angles and options. Point taken for the larger life picture as well as future photo ops.

In photography mode, I had gradually migrated to a spot fairly far away from Puma, who had patiently stayed in the down position while the world passed by him, including people with dogs (bless you, Cesar Millan!). Finally, Puma's protective genes clicked in, and he decided I was too far away to take proper care of and that I had forgotten the importance of that. Getting up, he walked over to where I was before again assuming the down position. Not picture-perfect obedience, but I could not argue with his logic.

Barred Owl sneaks a peek.

By this time, I felt I had plenty of photos of Owl with his eyes closed. Occasionally he peeked by opening one eye slightly, and I hoped against hope that he might open them fully. I tried asking him, to no avail. I considered sending Reiki to the situation but wondered if that would be selfish. Before I could resolve the debate, an unexpected event occurred; around the bend of the path came the local coon hound, one who could never resist greeting Puma by baying at him in ringing bugle tones, wanting to play. Puma stayed where he was, bless him, but the volume of the hound's voice caused Owl to finally open his eyes fully, looking downward to see what all the commotion was about. Owl did not look at all worried or disturbed, just mighty curious. I got several good shots before finally thanking Owl (and patient Puma) and taking my leave.

I returned to my schedule feeling uplifted and relaxed and realized that I needed to allow more time each day to consciously enjoy the gifts that can be found along the way, some of which come wrapped in feathers. On this particular day, I received a gift of Owl Medicine!

WILD MAN CHOOSES ME

This week, I again visited Mama Midnight and her six little black kittens, who were just six weeks old. When I arrived, Mama Midnight was nursing them, and they were an adorable pile of black fuzziness.

Eventually, Mama declared the milk bar closed, got up, and walked away, leaving the drowsy kittens wondering what to do next.

Gradually, they began to disperse for naps in nearby beds. But my guy, the kitten my guides had told me was to be mine before he was even born, came to me and began playing with my camera strap as he had the last time I visited.

He switched his attention to my right knee. After successfully scaling the heights, he rested on my leg and snuggled into my hand. As I spoke softly to him, he tilted his face upward, looking directly into my eyes as if what I was saying was the most important thing in the world. He was completely focused on me, and only me, and then he curled up against my hand and went to sleep.

We are definitely meant to be together.

ABOUT THE AUTHOR

Rose and her dog Puma (now in spirit).

Rose De Dan's work is inspired by wild and domestic animals who have issued a call to action for personal and global healing—truly a wild way to heal.

As an animal communicator, Reiki Master Teacher, and shamanic energy healer, Rose has encountered many animal teachers and healers. At their request, she builds bridges of connection and understanding between people and animals through storytelling, ceremonies, classes, sessions, photography, and art.

Rose resides in Seattle, Washington with her companion cats, who often appear in her stories. She also operates the Wild Reiki Spa and Wild Rose Cafe for the benefit of her wild neighbors whose antics can be seen on her YouTube channel.

VISIT ROSE'S WRSH WEBSITE

Website offers lots of goodies: stories, videos, photos, interviews, and other resources for animal lovers.

SIGN UP FOR THE NEWSLETTER

For more goodies: stories, upcoming books and class offerings!

Tap or scan to be taken to the WRSH website.

FIND WILD REIKI SHAMAN ON

Facebook

Instagram

Patreon

Threads

TikTok

Twitter (X)

YouTube

facebook.com/WildReikiShaman

instagram.com/wildreikishaman

patreon.com/wildreikishaman

threads.net/@wildreikishaman

tiktok.com/@wildreikishaman

x.com/wildreikishaman

youtube.com/@WildReikiShamanic

ALSO BY ROSE DE DAN

BOOKS

Tails of a Healer: Animals, Reiki and Shamanism

Out of the Darkness and Other Animal Tails

ANIMAL AND NATURE ART

Photo/Art Prints and Gifts by Rose De Dan

AUDIO/VIDEO

Storytelling for Animals and People

Whale Teachers

THANK YOU FOR READING!

If you enjoyed the stories, please consider posting a review. Reviews don't just help support authors, they help other readers discover our books. I also receive encouragement which makes me a happy storyteller (-:

Thanks in advance. May you have many amazing experiences of your own with All Our Relations!

Rose De Dan

www.ingramcontent.com/pod-product-compliance
Lightning Source LLC
Chambersburg PA
CBHW051203120626
46547CB00012B/1188